EDDIE:

THE LIFE AND TIMES OF AMERICA'S PREEMINENT BAD BOY

BY KEN OSMOND

AND CHRISTOPHER J. LYNCH

TABLE OF CONTENTS

ACKNOWLEDGEMENT

This book would not have been possible without the generous support of so many people who gave freely of their time through countless hours of interviews, numerous emails, and other correspondence. These individuals are listed here in alphabetical order:

Alice Cooper
Tony Dow
Steve Fischer
Henry Lane
Brian Levant
Jerry Mathers
Bob Mosher III
Christian Osmond
Dayton Osmond
Eric Osmond
Sandy Osmond
Kim Roderick
Harry Shearer

DEDICATION

This book is dedicated to my family, both immediate and extended.

To my parents, who, even though they raised me in the difficult time of post WWII years, provided a foundation of my personal values that have stood the test of time.

To Grandma and Grandpa, (Sandy's parents) for taking me in as one of their own. They were instrumental in my sons' becoming the best any father could hope for.

To Eric and Christian, my sons. I couldn't be more proud of them. They have become responsible adults. Both are professionals in their chosen endeavors.

To my wife Sandy, who has tolerated me through so many decades, and has been my partner in all the decisions that have brought us to our senior years, and a comfortable retirement.

Ken Osmond, 2014

Tony Dow as Wally Cleaver, circa 1958
"A kid like Eddie Haskell only comes along about once
in a couple hundred years."

Ken Osmond, circa 2014
"Nonsense; there's one on every block."

FOREWORD
By Jerry Mathers

Throughout the years, many people have asked me about Ken Osmond and if he really is like Eddie Haskell, who I think is one of the most memorable *Leave It to Beaver* characters. What I always say is, the real Ken Osmond is diametrically opposed to Eddie Haskell. He is nothing like him. Kenny is a great actor because he makes people believe that his personality is exactly like Eddie's. In reality, he is a devoted family man, very active in the American Legion, he loves to square dance, is a decorated police officer who was shot in the line of duty, and he is a wonderful friend.

I remember that when I had scenes with Kenny, he would always have his character and lines down, and he was the consummate professional. It was interesting to watch him, because other cast members on the show were pretty much like the people they portrayed in the series. Not that their personality was exactly the same, but for instance, Tony Dow was chosen because he was an Amateur Athletic Union swimming and diving champion, and he was very athletic much like his Wally character. Kenny was not chosen because he had a personality like Eddie Haskell, but because he was so good at acting like the two-faced, insincere kid that he portrayed as Eddie.

The character of Eddie Haskell is the ultimate nemesis in *Leave It to Beaver*. When you watch the show you have Ward and June, who are the parental authority figures, and they guide Beaver so he knows the difference between right and wrong. As the older brother, Wally always tried to counsel and protect the Beaver when he was about to do something impetuous or foolish, by explaining the consequences. Many times I did not listen to his advice! Then you have Eddie, who is the little devil on your shoulder whispering in your ear. He always tries to tempt the Beaver by telling him that his bad actions will not have any consequences, as he guides the Beaver in his version of the ways of the world. The character of Eddie is that person in our lives who always gets us into trouble. Everyone knows an "Eddie Haskell" and that's why the character is so easily recognized and remembered.

Some of my fondest memories while filming *Leave It to Beaver* were every once in a while, I was invited to go to lunch with Kenny, Tony Dow, and Frank Bank at the local drive-in restaurant, Bob's Big Boy, near our Universal Studios set. It was a really big treat if one of them would ask me to join the group. It would usually be Kenny who would say, "Oh yea, Jerry can come along with us." I felt very grateful to him, because it meant that I could hang out with the "big guys." Of course, in the very real life fashion of teenagers, and similar to their antics on *Leave It to Beaver*, the guys would sometimes make me hunch down in the backseat so that they could flirt with the girls and not be embarrassed that they had a little kid with them!

I have always been able to count on Kenny. When I

decided to buy a barbeque for my new house, Kenny asked me, "Have you ever built one before?"

"No," I said.

"I'll come over and help you," he replied.

Sure enough, the next day Kenny drove up to my house in his pickup truck which was full of bricks, sand, and cement. He showed me how to mix the cement, put the bricks up, and level them. And, in six hours, with a lot of laughs and a couple of beers, I had a brand new barbecue.

"Oh, we had a good day," remarked Kenny.

That's just the kind of friend he is.

Speaking in true Eddie Haskell form..."It's been a very lovely lifelong friendship we've had, Mr. Osmond."

Jerry Mathers
Actor, Director, Lecturer

P.S. Just another parting thought -- In real life, I was the oldest of five children in my family and Kenny only had one older brother. Ironically, in his family, he was really the Beaver. Who would have thought?

ONE
MORTIS INTERRUPTUS

September 20, 1980

LAPD Officer, Steve Fischer,
"Don't worry Kenny, you're gonna be fine, everything's
gonna be just fine."

The words were meant to reassure me, but I never in my life wanted to hear them, especially lying flat on my back, after being shot three times at point blank range. I knew what Steve was trying to do and I appreciated it. He and I had gone through the academy together a decade ago. Inches away from me, my assailant, who in legal parlance would still be referred to as *the suspect*, lie bleeding out, as the result of a single gunshot wound to the head. A river of blood flowed out of his cheek, down the sidewalk, and into the gutter. In the darkness of the night, the blood looked black, like crude oil. In the distance sirens were wailing, as every officer in the vicinity was racing to the call of: "Officer needs help – shots fired - officer down." I had done so myself in the past and joined in the screaming posse, I just never imagined they would be riding to me.

I stared up at Steve. He was a good cop, and a good man. I could trust him to do what I needed him to do next.

"I'm hurtin' real bad Steve," I said. "Tell my wife and my sons that I love 'em."

*   *   *

The night had begun as routinely as all the rest of them. My partner, Henry Lane, and I had done roll call and then stopped for dinner before beginning our evening shift on our motorcycles doing "Deuce Patrol." This was our cop shorthand for DUI (driving under the influence) and slang for the drunk drivers we were tasked with spotting and apprehending as our primary duty.

I loved working "motors" as it was called. In my ten years on the police department, it had been my favorite duty, far better than vice, or residential burglary. Part of the reason was because I loved motorcycles, and I had been an enthusiast my entire life, even to the point of taking cross-country tours with my wife, Sandy. Henry and I also had a special bond, as we had worked together for so many years.

I can't tell you how much I love Henry. You get closer to your partner than you do to your own spouse. You depend on them eight hours a day to save your life... and they do. Your partner is the most important thing in the world to you.

Our patrol area was in the Rampart Division of the LAPD jurisdiction. It was a tough, low-income neighborhood that was plagued by gang activity, drug dealing, and other violent crimes. Whether you were a cop or not, it was not an area where you could let your guard down if you wanted to survive.

I remember reading a study once that the average human makes a little over six hundred decisions per day. Most of these are benign judgment calls that have very little bearing on a person's safety or well-being: where to hang a bath towel, which shoe to tie first, what to eat, cash or credit, paper or plastic? As a police officer, I made all of the same decisions that an average person did - and then some very critical ones. Law enforcement is a profession like no other, a job where every "routine" traffic stop could be your last, and behind every door could be death. On the night of September 20, 1980, I made two life-altering decisions. One of these would be very good, and one of them would be very bad.

There had been a heat wave, and it had been hot all week in Los Angeles. Even in the evening, the lingering heat rose up from the blacktop and combined with the warm air that came off my Kawasaki air-cooled 1000cc motorcycle engine. Besides having to wear the standard, heavyweight uniform of the police department; in motors, we also had to wear a pair of knee-high "stove-pipe" boots, designed to keep our legs safe from road rash should we go down. Because of this, we postponed putting on our bulletproof vests as long as possible. We were supposed to have them on all the time, but I liked to push the rules a bit.

Finally, at about eleven o'clock at night, we stopped at a local fire station and went in to put on our vests. It felt like it always did to me, like I had wrapped my body in plastic.

The vest was a Morgan Magnum level II, manufactured by The Safariland Company. This was the standard issue for LAPD motor officers at the time, they were constructed of Kevlar and heavy canvas, and designed to stop a variety of handgun rounds. Without realizing it, I would be testing the limits of my vest tonight.

A little after midnight, we took up a post in a gas station parking lot on the corner of Alvarado and 8th Street and sat straddling the saddles of our bikes. It was one of our favorite hunting spots and we could usually count on at least a half dozen deuces a night from there. Just then, the radio crackled to life. A taxicab that had been stolen the previous day had just been spotted a couple blocks away. A few minutes after the call came in, we looked up and sure enough, there's the taxi with the correct numbers on the side. So we called it in, and fired up our scooters.

We fell in behind the vehicle and followed him for just a short distance, westbound on 8th Street. Before we could even switch on our lights to get his attention and pull him over, the guy pulled over to the curb on his own accord. Henry rolled up to the rear of the cab on the driver's side and dismounted. I rode my motorcycle up onto the sidewalk on the passenger's side and dismounted as well. Since it was a stolen vehicle, we both drew our guns.

> *Henry Lane,*
> *"We both walked up to the car and he's (the suspect) writing something in a book. Evidently he stole this cab the day before and had been running around the city picking up fares. (Laughing) I guess he found himself a real job."*

I aimed my gun into the open passenger window of the cab, lined up the sights on the guy inside and yelled, "Freeze!" He floored the accelerator and the vehicle took off with a squeal of tires. Our investigative stop had now become a high-speed pursuit. The chase was on.

We remounted our bikes, activated the sirens, and called in an official pursuit. A short distance away, at

Rampart Street, the taxi turned sharply to the right, clipping a car parked on the right-hand side of the street, and then careened toward the opposite side, striking another. This guy was dead set on escaping, and didn't even slow down. He made another sharp right onto 7th Street, the rear wheels of the cab fish-tailing all over the place. A few blocks later, he turned again, and skidded left onto Coronado Street. This time, when he turned onto Coronado, he crashed into another parked car so violently he disabled the cab. With no car left, he took off on foot.

The suspect sprinted toward a large apartment building on the west side of the street, ducked into a driveway, and headed toward the rear. Henry and I stayed mounted on our motorcycles and just followed him until he ran out of room.

At the rear of the building, the driveway turned to the north and then circled around to another driveway on the far side of the building. The driveway essentially surrounded the apartment in a giant "U" shape. By now, the suspect had crossed the back of the building and was heading eastbound down the second driveway, and back toward the front of the building and Coronado Street. At the end of the driveway, a heavy chain was suspended a couple feet above the concrete, blocking any vehicles. Henry and I knew we were screwed as far as following him on our bikes any longer and would have to pick it up on foot. What neither of us knew however, was that the chain was the least of our worries tonight. The situation was about to get much worse.

Henry Lane
"At the end of the driveway, I thought he was just going to jump the chain and keep running. But then he spun around, and I saw a six-inch, blue-steel revolver sticking out of his waistband. His hand

was on it."

Realizing that the suspect had a gun, Henry dismounted his motorcycle and let it continue forward. The forward momentum of the bike struck the suspect hard and knocked him over the chain. He got up and took off running across the street.

I dumped my bike, jumped the chain, and took off after him along with Henry. Then I heard my partner yell out, "Shoot him!"

I knew at that point, that Henry knew something that I didn't know - something very bad. I trusted my partner indubitably, and I wasn't about to question his judgment. I pulled my service revolver out to shoot at the suspect, but Henry had gotten ahead of me, blocking my shot. Henry was firing and winged the guy a couple of times. The guy would fall, but then he'd get up again and keep running. Then Henry ran out of bullets. He tried to reload as he ran, but our weapons back then were old .38 revolvers, and we didn't have "speed-loaders." It was awkward and slowing my partner down. I knew it was all up to me. I sped past Henry and ran after the suspect.

The suspect reached the corner of 7th Street and turned to the left, heading eastbound. I wasn't far behind him. Then a short distance up the street, he turned left again, into the opening of what I thought was another apartment building. I'll admit that it was poor tactics on my part that I thought he had continued running into the building, when in fact, he had stopped and was waiting for me. Then I turned the corner, and all I saw were flashes of light; I never even heard the gunfire.

Three .38 caliber rounds slammed into me at point blank-range; one in the upper chest, one in the lower chest, and one in the lower abdomen. We were standing only inches apart from one another in the tiny doorway of an office building west of downtown LA. The door to the building was locked, so the guy just waited for me to catch up. Stupid, stupid, stupid on my part.

I didn't realize it at the time, but I had gotten off three rounds as well. One went high and took out the glass door behind him. Two bullets hit the suspect, one in the left forearm, and one in the "love handle." It wouldn't be enough to stop him.

The force of the suspect's rounds hit me like sledgehammer blows, knocking me backward. And the next thing I realized, I was flat on my back on the sidewalk and I couldn't move. I was still cognizant of my surroundings and what was going on, but nothing on my body worked; I was totally paralyzed!

The suspect must have realized he had an opportunity, because he got up and walked over to where I was laying on the sidewalk. Very calmly, he put the muzzle of his gun to my forehead. Later on, I would learn that the guy was a career criminal who had murdered before. He had killed his girlfriend on her twenty-seventh birthday by stabbing her to death twenty-seven times. Killing a cop with just a few pounds of trigger pull would be nothing to him. He squeezed the trigger on the double-action revolver and the hammer drew back.

In some of my many movie roles, I'd been killed on the silver screen. But this wasn't acting, and the bullets in the suspect's gun weren't blanks. It was at this moment that I realized my life would be ending. I was getting the coup de grâce.

Just then, in the nick of time, Henry caught up to us. He stuck his hand between the hammer and the frame of the gun and prevented it from firing. He wrestled the suspect off of me and onto the ground next to me. The suspect's revolver still had three rounds remaining in it, and he and Henry were fighting for control of the gun.

In the meantime, I was still unable to move, and for

some crazy reason, my service revolver had made it into my left hand, opposite my shooting hand. I figured that I might still have rounds remaining. Henry and the suspect were wrestling just inches away from me, and I can remember looking down my left arm and seeing that my gun was pointed at the guy's head. And I tried...oh, I tried so hard to pull the trigger, but I just couldn't do it. My fingers just wouldn't move! Then, I heard another shot ring out.

While Henry and the suspect were struggling, the guy's gun discharged just under his (the suspect's) chin. Luckily for the bad guy, the bullet's angle didn't send it directly up into his brain cavity. Instead, it hit his mandible, ricocheted off of it, and took out his larynx. He would have to miss choir practice for a while. Blood started gushing out of his head onto the sidewalk, draining into the gutter.

By the time other officers and medical personnel got to the scene, I had begun to regain motor control. In addition to the quick and heroic actions of Henry, my life had been spared by my equipment - even my uniform. The bulletproof vest that I'd been so loathe to put on that night, had stopped the rounds that struck my upper and lower chest. But my belt buckle stopped the most lethal shot of all; the one aimed at my lower abdomen. The slug had hit the wide metal part of the buckle, bending it inward by more than an inch. According to the medical personnel who examined me later, if the bullet had gone one half of an inch either way, I would have most likely died from my wounds.

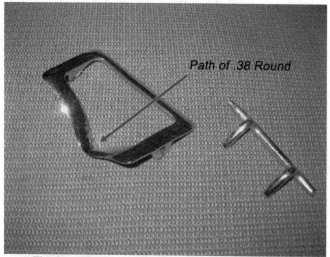

The damaged buckle from my standard issue police belt.
This tiny piece of metal stopped the most lethal of the rounds from
penetrating my body.

Amazingly, my assailant survived as well. In fact, we had to share an ambulance ride to the hospital together. I was angry with that, but what really ticked me off is that the case never went to trial. The district attorney took the path of least resistance and ignored all of the other crimes the guy committed that night: grand theft auto, possession of a stolen firearm by a convicted felon, hit and run, evading arrest, and attempted murder. In the end, it was plea-bargained down to a single charge of section 245D of the California Penal Code, *Assault with a firearm against a peace officer.* Not until almost a year later, was the guy finally sent into the California state prison system to begin serving his sentence.

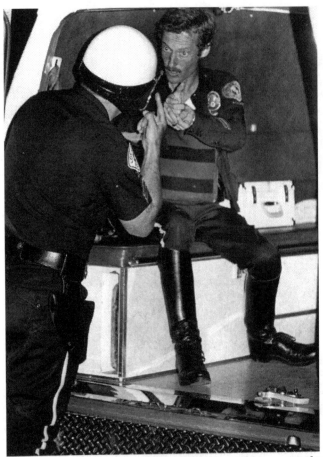

Post shooting and inside the ambulance waiting to be transported to the hospital.

In all, the car chase covered less than one mile, with the entire encounter occurring in less than five minutes. They were life-changing moments, and the outcome could have gone either way. A man had attempted, unsuccessfully, to end my life. So dramatic was the story, it was later made into an episode for the television show, *Top Cops*.

To Ken,

MY, THAT'S A REAL NICE SHIRT YOU HAVE ON MR. OSMOND!!

Your Pal Sonny

With Sonny Grosso, the executive producer of Top Cops. A former NYPD policeman, he was one of the two detectives immortalized in the 1971 movie, "The French Connection."

A little more than one month later, I was back at work with the LAPD. I did desk duty while I waited for my shoulder, injured in the shooting, to heal sufficiently. It did, and before long, I was cleared for full duty and was back to patrolling the mean streets of Los Angeles with my trusted partner Henry Lane, the man to whom I owe my life.

But it wasn't just my life as a cop, or as a husband, or a father, that my partner had helped save that hot night in September 1980. It was another part of my life, a life that seemed so long ago. It was the part of my life that I had abandoned years prior, thinking I would never return to it.

While my assailant was cooling his heels in the state penitentiary, I had returned to Universal Studios. It was time to return to my old life, time to revive my role as Eddie Haskell in *The New Leave It to Beaver* television series.

Eddie Haskell Trivia Chapter 1: In one of his many "deaths" on the silver screen, a young Ken Osmond lay stricken as the victim of an auto accident. A priest, played by a popular leading man of the time, cradled him in his arms and kissed him good-bye. Who was that leading man?
Answer at the end of Chapter 2

TWO
EXODUS

Besides the requisite name and dates, there are three words engraved on my father's headstone: "A Good Man." They were added to the stone for a very simple reason; my father was a good man.

His name was Thurman, and my mother's name was Pearl. My father had been born in Texas, my mother, Oklahoma, although both had been raised in Oklahoma. This was back when it was an accomplishment just to stay alive. They had survived the twin blows of the dustbowl and the great depression. And anyone who could do that was tough...very tough.

My father was of only average height and build, but he was of formidable integrity and character. These were the qualities that would guide me through life. As a young man growing up, my father had to travel extensively just to put what meager food he could on the family's table. He and my grandfather would ride the rails to find what little work that they could. They would hop onto a freight car and keep their eyes open for any fields or orchards that needed picking. When they saw one, they would jump off the train. They didn't even know where they were half the time.

My mother had it even worse.

Pearl Osmond (nee Hand) was one of 13 children, only 11 of whom survived to adulthood. Once, when the Red Cross came to check on my mom's family, they found them living in total squalor in a dugout under a tree. One of her brothers had managed to kill a sparrow, and my grandma was cooking it in order to keep the youngest child alive. Now that was poverty.

In 1941 my parents decided to move west to find a better life. World War II had just begun, and a lot of the airplane manufacturing plants were located in Southern California. Besides that, there was also the movie industry, although that seemed like a fanciful dream at the time.

They had been living in Gotebo, Oklahoma, a hardscrabble town that was located southwest of the center of the state. Rumor had it that it had once briefly been in the running to become the state capital. Despite this distinction, and the fact that two major railroads intersected the town, it still couldn't escape the harsh economic realities the dustbowl and the depression had created.

Nearly 2.5 million people had already escaped the plains states and moved west by the time my parents left. I guess mom and pop decided that they weren't going to be the only ones left to turn the lights out on poor old Gotebo. Besides that, they had my older brother Dayton to look after, and they didn't want him to have the same hand-to-mouth existence they had suffered through. So in 1941, they lashed their feather mattress onto the roof of their dilapidated '32 Ford and packed what meager belongings they owned into it. They pointed the car westward, on an historic old road by the name of Route 66.

Four arduous days later they arrived in California, tired, dirty and broke. They had only 65 cents to their name, and were not able to afford even the most basic of accommodations. The owner of a small hotel took pity on them and allowed them to sleep on the back patio of the building for fifty cents that night. They unloaded their prized mattress, tossed it onto the ground, and the three of them collapsed on top of it. This was their welcome to the Promised Land.

* * *

Unlike the fictional Joad family from *The Grapes of Wrath*, my parents didn't head for California's rich agricultural heartland in the San Joaquin Valley; they had already had their fill of backbreaking farm work. The San Fernando Valley north of Los Angeles had been on a growth spurt ever since water began flowing into it from the California Aqueduct a few decades earlier. This in turn led to a housing boom, and that meant job opportunities. Pop quickly found work in a nearby lumberyard, but he only stayed on for a month before moving on to bigger and better things.

Vega Aircraft was a subsidiary of Lockheed, and was located in Burbank, not far from where my family lived. In conjunction with Boeing and Douglas Aircraft, Vega built the famous B-17. Even though the factory operated 24/7, the plant could barely keep up with the war demand for the plane known colloquially as "The Flying Fortress." The bottom line was; if you could fog a mirror, you could find work at Vega.

Both of my parents got jobs there, and they were able to work alternating shifts to cover the duties of parenting my brother; Pop would work the day shift and my mom would work the night. Besides aerospace manufacturing, my father also found lucrative, albeit sporadic, employment as a carpenter at nearby Universal Studios.

> *Dayton Osmond,*
> *"This was before the unions had made a foothold*
> *into the movie studios, and so a bunch of men*
> *would go sit down in the dry river bottom every day*
> *waiting for work. A foreman would come out onto*
> *the dock and say, 'I need four men; you, you,*
> *you...and you. And that was it. If you didn't get*
> *picked, you didn't work."*

It was a good thing my father was able to find lots of work, because in the fall of 1942 my mom had to quit working at Vega aircraft; she was pregnant with me.

* * *

I was born on June 7, 1943 at the Glendale Sanitarium in Los Angeles County. I was told that at the time, you could see the Colorado Street Bridge in Pasadena from the hospital. You may have heard of this bridge by another name: "Suicide Bridge." More than a hundred people were reported to have leapt to their death by taking the one hundred fifty foot one-way plunge to the Arroyo Seco riverbed below. Most of these occurred during the depression. They've since redone the bridge to include "anti-suicide" barriers and other impediments, and of course, there's a bunch of urban myths about ghosts and hauntings. They even have an annual suicide bridge celebration. I always thought it was ironic that I came into the world not far from where a lot of people departed it.

My family lived in a small house on Forman Street in the bedroom community of Toluca Lake. It was the same town where Bob Hope lived and was just north of Universal Studios. I don't remember anything about this house because we didn't stay there very long; the family plans were about to change. It was 1945 and I was two years old.

* * *

I guess my parents had grown homesick for a simpler life, and with the family coffers swollen from several years of steady employment, Pop must have felt he had the grubstake he needed to change the direction of our family's fortune. Once again, we loaded the '32 Ford – now nicknamed "Bunky" and got back onto Route 66. But this time, we headed east.

We landed in Mansfield, Missouri where my pop bought a dairy farm along with some hogs. Our next door neighbor was none other than Laura Ingalls-Wilder, the author of "The Little House on the Prairie" series of books. The Ingalls-Wilder family members were very nice people. Pop had a .22 rifle, but it wasn't good for much since the barrel was bent and it couldn't shoot straight. The Ingalls-Wilder family used to loan their gun to my dad so he could go hunt squirrels and have something to show for it.

I was too young to go hunting with Pop, but my brother Dayton and I used to go exploring a lot. A short distance from our family farm was a natural cave, set into the side of the hills. We used to go spelunking there with my cousins Gene and "Corky" (Bonnie). I remember that it narrowed the further in we went, and we would have to get down on our hands and knees to keep going as far as we did. Since I was just barely out of diapers and the littlest, I used to get to go in further than the rest of them.

With Dayton and Pop back in Missouri.

As much fun as this Tom Sawyer life was for a couple of young boys, the farming was far greater work than the rewards it reaped. After only a year in Missouri, we packed up once again and headed back to California. It would be the last big move we would ever make in our lives.

I'm sure at the time my pop might have thought that moving back was a big disappointment for my mom. But for a young woman who had seen so many struggles in her life, the move back to the suburbs of the San Fernando Valley didn't represent defeat as much as the opportunity she never thought possible growing up. The war would be ending soon, and with it, the motion picture industry would be getting back on track. Her dreams for Dayton and I were far more ambitious than to see us become successful livestock ranchers. She was going to make us into stars.

Eddie Haskell Trivia Answer Chapter 1
The movie was Battle Hymn, and the actor that
kissed Ken Osmond as he lay dyeing was Rock
Hudson.

Eddie Haskell Trivia Chapter 2: Gotebo, Oklahoma
never did achieve the title of state capital, but what
is its claim to fame?
Answer at the end of Chapter 3

THREE
SHOW TIME!

My mother was what you would call a real 'stage mom.' She was always hustling my brother, Dayton, and I off to various lessons and interviews for parts. I think she was living vicariously through us. We had just barely gotten back to California and had settled into our new home on Hesby Street in North Hollywood, before she began what was to become a lifelong quest for her.

It was 1947, and with the war over, the good jobs in the aerospace industry had dried up considerably. In the meantime, a union, the IATSE (International Alliance of Theatrical Stage Employees) Local 44, had been established at the various movie studios. With my pop's experience, he was able to gain membership to the union and enjoy steady work for the princely sum of $125.00 per week. He became a prop maker and a set-builder. He would work at this job for the rest of his life.

I remember that Pop worked mostly at Universal Studios, which was pretty close to our house. We would drive by there from time to time on our way to lessons or interviews, and I would point to it and say, "That's where my daddy's shop is."

Besides making small items in the studio's mill, he would do work on the studio back lot, building sets for everything from dramas, to westerns, to high sea adventures. Without any of us realizing it, this was to mark the beginning of the Osmond's lifetime of financial dependency on the entertainment industry. Before long, everyone in our family would be connected to the studios in one form or another.

In the meantime, at the tender age of four, before I had yet to attend a day of kindergarten at nearby Lankershim Elementary School, I began taking lessons, along with Dayton, in the various disciplines of entertainment. The first of these instructions were drama classes, and the instructor's name was Cosmo Morgan.

Besides having a very unique name, Mr. Morgan was an interesting character. I got the impression, even at my young age, that he probably had independent money and that teaching acting to children was the love of his life. He owned an actual Gutenberg Bible, which is virtually priceless, and he had it on loan to a museum in England.

Besides drama, he also taught us diction and dialects. Dayton was able to read a little, but I had yet to learn, and so we practiced and performed without the benefit of scripts. I remember doing mock plays that Mr. Morgan would create, and then we would be evaluated for our performance. The work taught us at an early age the very foundations from which performance emerges.

After the lessons, it would be back to the house on Hesby Street where we lived like every other blue-collar family. It was a small house on a very narrow lot that was only forty feet wide. Several units sat at the back of the property and were rented to other tenants; we rented the front house. The house was strictly bare-bones and had no furnace, only a small gas fitting that protruded from the wall that could be connected to a small, portable heater.

One of the things we could see from our house was Mount Wilson, to the east of us. When I was about four years old, they had constructed the first antennae on the summit to begin broadcasting for a local TV station, KTLA Channel 5. There were only about three hundred fifty TV sets in all of Los Angeles when the station went live, but the number was growing rapidly. I had no idea, looking up at the summit of Mount Wilson that in just a year or so, my image would be broadcast from it.

On Vineland Boulevard, not far from our house, was the Western District light rail section of the famous Pacific Electric Red Car line. Before it was summarily bought up and destroyed by a consortium made up of General Motors, Firestone Tire, and the Standard Oil Company, it was one of the first forms of mass transit in car crazy Los Angeles. This section of the narrow-gauge tracks carried riders all the way from the city of San Fernando through North Hollywood, past Universal Studios, and then into Hollywood. My mom wanted desperately to hitch her wagon to something to get Dayton and me to Hollywood, but it wasn't going to be a streetcar that took us there.

* * *

Lola Moore was legendary in the entertainment industry as being the go-to person for children's talent. Each year, she produced her *Junior Artist Directory*, a "Wish Book" of sorts that catalogued pictures and stats on every one of her clients – and she had plenty! She held a virtual monopoly on young talent, and represented many of the up and coming child stars of the day: Paul Peterson, John Provost, Shelly Fabares, and Angela Cartwright. Her agency was a self-fulfilling prophecy because the more talent she signed, the more she booked. And the more work she booked, the more talent she signed. The bottom line was; if you were a producer or director looking for young talent, you went to Lola. It also meant that if your son or daughter wanted to get noticed, they had to be a part of her prestigious stable.

Around the same time I started kindergarten, my mom went to work for Lola Moore as a secretary and receptionist. I think it was considered to be a *gratis* sort of arrangement between them, so my mom collected little to no salary. But, as the ambitious stage mother to two budding entertainment hopefuls, it was a sacrifice she was more than willing to make in order to get as close as possible to the legendary talent agent. Working for Lola meant that my mom had an inside track to plum auditions, as well as to gaining knowledge about charting the proper development path for Dayton and myself. For a dedicated housewife and mother, it was a large investment of time, but it was a shrewd strategy that would soon begin to pay dividends.

My page from Lola Moore's "wish book" of young talent.

My mom learned quickly from Lola the cardinal sin of the "One-Trick Pony." Dayton and I could not get many doors opened for us if we were to be strictly trained in dramatics alone. We needed depth, and new skills, such as dancing and musicianship.

Before long, we were taking lessons in a variety of disciplines. Dayton learned to play the accordion, and we both took dance lessons, tap at first, then ballroom, ballet, minuet, and even square dancing!

My square dancing outfit had been designed by none other than the famous costume designer, Nuta Kotlyarenko, known locally as "Nudie" Cohn, at his tailor shop on the corner of Victory and Vineland in North Hollywood. Nudie was quite a character. He was the first guy to ever put rhinestones on cowboy outfits, and he made them for all the famous cowboys of stage and screen. He also had a passion for outrageous cars and always drove big old Pontiac convertibles with steer horns on the front.

Our square dancing group. I'm third from the left.

In addition to our lessons, we also began to go on interviews for parts in plays and musicals. Lola Moore had told my mom that performing mock plays for an instructor was one thing, but standing on stage in front of an audience was another.

"Your boys need to rack up some show time," she said.

In many cases, these interviews were strictly "cattle-calls," with every kid in town at them, along with their stage moms.

Dancing the minuet.

In spite of the stiff competition, we began booking performances at small venues, and even some larger ones, such as The Pasadena Playhouse and Grauman's Chinese Theatre. The Burbank Theatre, close to where we lived in North Hollywood, was considered to be one of the more prominent live theaters left in Los Angeles. The obituary on vaudeville had been officially written a decade earlier, but no one had bothered to tell the

Burbank Theatre, and the historic venue could still pack them in for song and dance variety shows.

Big crowds notwithstanding, virtually none of these performances paid anything. I do remember though that at the end of the shows, the master of ceremonies would often ask the audience to help support the young entertainers, and people would throw pennies, and sometimes nickels, up onto the stage. All of us kids would scamper around like crazy to pick up as much as we could, because in those days, it was a lot of money.

We had one very memorable performance during the 1948 *Burbank on Parade*, which seemed to be designed as a promotional vehicle for the city. It consisted of an extensive talent show, and a Miss Burbank Beauty Pageant where every entrant received a new blouse and a scarf. That year, sharing the same stage with us, was a young ingenue by the name of Mary Frances Reynolds, who took the crown. Besides bragging rights and a trip to New York, Warner Brothers Studios also gave her a screen test. She impressed them enough that she was given a seven-year contract. She became the award winning singer and actress, Debbie Reynolds.

It was around this time, when I was five or six years old, that I got my first break in television. It was on one of the many live shows that were springing up on the local Los Angeles channels. This one was called *Grandma Moses,* and it was broadcast on KHJ-TV, Channel 9. The show employed a formula later perfected by such TV legends as Art Linkletter, and Allen Funt of *Candid Camera*. Basically it was built around an elderly woman who played Grandma Moses. She would have all of us kids sitting around her and then she would ask us questions, hoping for an outrageous answer; kind of along the lines of 'out of the mouths of babes, oft times come gems.' In reality though, it was pretty much scripted. We would already know what she was going to ask and we would have set answers to recite back to her. To be fair though, live television was the equivalent of a trapeze artist working without a net, and children could be unpredictable.

Besides variety acts and local television, I also performed in dramatic stage plays. My live dramatic debut was *Goodbye Again* at the Beverly Hills Playhouse. I learned later that live drama was important for the resume of a developing actor, but it wasn't something I enjoyed doing. It wasn't stage fright or anything like that, it just wasn't my bag, I guess you could say.

On the set of Grandma Moses.

In between all of the endless lessons, rehearsals, interviews, and performances, Dayton and I still managed to maintain a fairly normal childhood. Although we had our tussles like any normal brothers – Dayton once hit me on the head with a judge's gavel -

our brotherly bond was growing. Every Saturday we would walk the half-mile or so to the local movie theatre to see the latest double feature. During the summertime, it was a walk to the local public pool where we would swim all day for five cents. I'd have to say that I really loved growing up when I did. It was a great time to be a kid. It wasn't exactly as pristine as the Cleavers on *Leave It to Beaver*, but it was still really good. I can't imagine growing up as a kid these days.

I also never resented my mom for all of the lessons and interviews she had us go to. To me, this was just something that you did as a kid growing up. I didn't know any better and just thought, 'Isn't this what every kid does?' I guess I was just too young and innocent to know any differently.

As plentiful as the work that Dayton and I were doing with live variety shows and drama, it still wasn't getting us any closer to making it onto the silver screen; we obviously needed more arrows in our quivers. Lola Moore advised my mom that we needed to be much more than just another couple of cute kids who could tap dance and play a musical instrument.

"Film requires talents of an even broader spectrum," Lola said.

Pretty soon, we were heading off to still more lessons – if that was even humanly possible. We began augmenting our dance and stage drama talents with classes in fencing, martial arts, and horseback riding. It was something you learned pretty quickly going on interviews; if they asked you if you could ride a horse, you answered, "Yes, I can certainly ride a horse." Then you'd leave the interview and after you heard you got the job, you'd run out and take riding lessons.

This was a spec ad that likely never got shown.

Just unpacked new shipment of sport shirts. Sanforized cotton flannels, ginghams, solid color linenweave rayons. Sizes 6-18.

(d) 100% nylon jackets
REG. 12.95

8.99

Travis nylon, nylon fleece lined in winter white. A cinch to launder, they require no ironing. Sizes 4-12.
Prep sizes 14-18, reg. 13.95
9.99

(e) wash 'n' wear slacks
REG. 10.95

8.99

65% Dacron-35% acetate gabardine slacks you can wash in machine, drip dry, have ready to wear smooth and creased without stroke of ironing. Sizes 10-18.

(f) cotton tee shirts
REG. 1.69

3/4.00 **1.39**

Combed cotton in new chartones, navy, red and brown stripings. Sizes 6-16.
(g) 2.98 "may boy" guaranteed knee jeans; 4-12

In the May Company ad, pushing cotton tee shirts.

Another thing we did was print modeling. Besides actually bringing in a little money to pay for all of the lessons and outfits, it also gave us exposure. I appeared in a spec ad for Kellogg's Sugar Pops, and we did lots of fashion work for the high-end May Company Department Store. My mom would take Dayton and me on the Red Line to downtown Los Angeles to the only May Company store in town. We would go to a photography studio upstairs from the department store, and they would have us model clothes and take pictures of us. The next week, we would be in the sales ad in the paper.

All of this work: the endless lessons, the interviews, the stage plays, the modeling, came down to one very important phone call. I remember that it was 1949, and Dayton and I were playing in the backyard of our house when the phone rang inside. My mom came rushing out after a few minutes and pulled us really close to her. Her voice was very excited, the kind of voice you would have if you had just had a lifelong dream come true.

"Boys," she said. "That was MGM on the phone; you're going to be in the movies."

Eddie Haskell Trivia Answer Chapter 2
Gotebo, Oklahoma never became the state capital,
but it does have the dubious distinction as the
"Goat-Ropin' Capital of the World."

Eddie Haskell Trivia Chapter 3: Besides making
outfits for cowboys and rodeo stars, Nudie Cohn
also made one very special $10,000 gold lamé suit
for one legendary performer. Who was that
performer?
Answer at the end of Chapter 4

FOUR
PLYMOUTH ADVENTURE

The title of the first movie Dayton and I ever performed in was *Plymouth Adventure*. It was MGM's 1952 epic seafaring tale of the voyage of the Pilgrims on the Mayflower in 1620. Like a lot of the big films of the time, it was filmed in Technicolor, and it had an ensemble cast that included Spencer Tracy, Gene Tierney, and Van Johnson. The film won the Oscar that year for special effects for its use of a 1/3-scale model of the Mayflower in action sequences.

But in spite of the impressive credentials of the cast members, and the prestigious award, the film, like many of the time, still lost money – at least according to the studio's Byzantine accounting practices!

From the end of World War II, and into the first part of the 1950s, the Hollywood studios found themselves caught in a tailspin. Theatre revenues had remained high during the war years, and box office sales had set an all time high record in 1947. But after that time, the receipts had fallen precipitously as moviegoers stayed away in droves. Several factors contributed to the drop, and outraged studio executives were looking for scapegoats. They did not have to look very hard.

Going all the way back to the silent era, the studios had owned the movie houses that showed their films lock, stock, and barrel.. But in 1948, a Supreme Court ruling known as the *Paramount Decision* forced the studios to divest themselves of their theatre chains. Without the studios able to exercise virtual monopolies in this final link in the distribution chain, theatres could now be choosier about what they wanted to show, and for how long. For the studios, who were used to cranking out a steady stream of formulaic "B" movies and then using their muscle to force theatres to show them, this meant a growing backlog of films "in the can" that had yet to find a venue. We wrapped the production of *Plymouth Adventure* in 1950, yet the movie was not released until a full two years later.

Still another convenient target to assign blame for the dearth of box office receipts, was none other than television itself. Since the major networks had begun regular broadcasting in the 1940s, television had slowly and steadily continued its march into American homes, and soon became the new way of life. The convenience and novelty offered by the entertainment that streamed for free out of the "magic box" was like a parasite that was eating the studios' lunch. This erosion of their - up until this point - nearly guaranteed revenue stream, was something that gave the movie moguls fits, and became, for the industry, a source of much derision and outright contempt. I remember hearing that insufferable Jack Warner would terminate any employee if they so much as included a TV in the set of any of the Warner Brothers' movies.

But Dayton and I were oblivious to all of the battles – real or imagined – that raged around us as our mom drove us down to the MGM lot in Culver City that spring morning in 1950. For three months we were shuttled back and forth to the landmark studio. Our work was mostly as extras, with the occasional few lines of ad-lib dialogue thrown in for good measure. But it was our first movie production, and we were able to experience firsthand the magic that brought stories onto the silver screen.

A majority of the scenes were shot on a huge sound stage that contained a full-scale model of the Mayflower which was cut in half to allow for above-deck and below-deck scenes. Not having the luxury of CGI (computer generated imagery) or automation, stage workers known as grips wedged huge timbers under the hull and would push and pull on them to simulate the rocking action of the seas. During the violent storm scenes, buckets of lukewarm water would be tossed from down below the rails, dousing us as we stood on the decks. I remember one especially dramatic scene, when a huge beam that supported the deck above it was rigged to break, and all of this water was supposed to come pouring down on us. It was pretty exciting to see all of the work that went into the scene. The beam had to break at just the right moment, so everything had to go perfect the very first time.

Even though we weren't in them, the special effects outdoor scenes were really fun to watch the crew film. The scenes showing the ship traversing the water were shot using the 1/3 scale model of the Mayflower, towed by an underwater cable on a man-made lake on the MGM back lot. Off to one side of the lake, they had all of these barrels in the water, mounted on a long pole that they rotated. The barrels were offset, so when they turned the pole, it created the waves that appear in the movie.

Besides all the elaborate sets and the special effects, we had to look like the parts we were playing as well. In addition to our authentic costuming, this meant that our hairstyles had to fit the period as well. My mom had been instructed by the studio not to cut our hair for the entire time of the shooting. I remember we had to wear a "fall" or mock hairpiece in the beginning until our own real hair could grow out. Our hair got very long over the three months we were shooting. Remember that this was the early fifties, and that there were no Beatles - or even Elvis yet, so long hair on boys was just not something you ever saw. On the weekends that we were not working, this created some unique situations.

> *Dayton Osmond,*
> *"Our hair was so long, when we went down to the pool to swim, nobody recognized us. In fact, they didn't even recognize us as being boys and told us to get into the line for girls. We had to prove ourselves otherwise."*

There were about five or six other boys who acted with us in *Plymouth Adventure*. One of these was Tommy *"TV Tommy"* Ivo, who played William Button, the only passenger who died during the Mayflower's historic crossing. Years later Ivo would go on to become a successful drag racer. Before he made the move to motor sports, Ivo's acting roles included playing Shelly Fabares' boyfriend on *The Donna Reed Show*. Unbeknownst to either one of us, Tom and I would work together again on the *Leave It to Beaver* show a couple of years later.

Ivo was also one of the cast members who came to my house for my eighth birthday party. My parents had bought a larger house over on Willowcrest in North Hollywood, and Ivo came over, along with a bunch of other cast and crewmembers for my party. One very important cast member couldn't make it to the house that day, but he still went out of his way to be nice to me on the set.

Believe it or not, one of the things I remember most about working on *Plymouth Adventure* was that it was the first time I ever had a box lunch, which I thought was pretty special. One time when I was eating, a man came over, sat down next to me, and started talking. I knew he was one of the other actors from the movie, but I didn't know who he was, or how important. Later on, I realized I had lunch with Spencer Tracy!

After *Plymouth Adventure* wrapped and went into postproduction, Dayton and I went back to regular school, returning to the grind of our specialized classes and interviews. *Plymouth Adventure* was the last time Dayton and I would ever perform together. Now that we had a feature film credit under our belts, our resumes looked more impressive, and work started coming to each of us with greater frequency and magnitude. We never had to perform campy vaudeville acts on stage for pocket change any longer. Just a few months after Plymouth wrapped, I was already heading to Warner Brothers Studios in Burbank. Lola Moore had gotten me another movie role.

Eddie Haskell Trivia Answer Chapter 3
Nudie Cohn, who sewed all of Ken Osmond's
square dancing outfits, made a $10,000 gold lamé
suit for "The King" himself, Elvis Presley.

Eddie Haskell Trivia Chapter 4: A one third scale
model of the Mayflower was built for the special
effect scenes in Plymouth Adventure. What
happened to that model? Answer at the end of
Chapter 5

FIVE
THE GOLDEN AGE OF TELEVISION

So Big was the 1953 Warner Brothers feature-length production of Edna Ferber's classic novel about struggle, disappointment, and redemption. Jane Wyman starred in the movie, and is credited with carrying it. My role in the film was as young Eugene. It was my first speaking role in a film, but it was very small role *and* I was un-credited – which was common for the time. Whoever said, "There are no small roles, only small actors," was full of it. I know, because I've had plenty of small roles.

Still, I was an actor and it was work. You took whatever role you got and were grateful for it. It was also work that, like *Plymouth Adventure*, would pad my resume as well as expand my circle of peers with whom I would later get to work with.

In the *So Big* production with me, were two other child actors who would each go on to have major roles in one of television's most endearing shows from the 1950s and '60s. Tommy Rettig and Jon Provost would each play opposite America's favorite collie, Lassie, in the television show of the same name. Rettig would star as Jeff Miller from 1954 to 1957, and Provost would play Timmy Martin from 1957 to 1964. I would get to play alongside each of them throughout *Lassie's* long run. This was not a unique circumstance.

In the industry, and especially at the time, it was pretty common to run into people you knew. You'd see them at interviews, or maybe you'd work with them here or there. Off set, your paths crossed as well.

I remember playing baseball in the neighborhood with Michael Winkelman, who played Little Luke on the TV show *The Real McCoys*. He lived about a half block away from where we lived in North Hollywood. There were lots of kid actors in TV and movies, and it was pretty much a way of life for us back then. Unlike today's child actors, nobody thought we were anything special.

The connection to other young performers in television production, and to television itself, was no fluke as this medium was to become the major force in my career from this point on. By 1953, the number of households that had television sets had grown to over twenty million, or about 45%. My image would soon be one of the many beamed into half of America's living rooms. The movie studios, in spite of their initial resistance to television, and their repugnance to what it represented, this equivalent of "fast food" entertainment had begun to get accepted as a fait accompli. No doubt the major studio heads still resented TV due to their lack of absolute control over it, but they had to get onboard lest the early adopters of the technology such as Disney and Desilu took over while they were busy wringing their hands. Ever the stubborn one, Warner Brothers wouldn't cry "uncle" until 1955 when they finally got into television production.

Part of the reason for TV's meteoritic rise during this era was the growing cold war between the US and its erstwhile, and some would say – dubious - ally against the Germans in WWII; the Russians. After successfully exploding a nuclear bomb in 1949, the world's communist superpower had ramped up its rhetoric and was craftily orchestrating a proxy battle between a divided Korean nation as a way to further their agenda.

As this conflict raged just an ocean away, children in American schools practiced "drop and cover" drills in the event of nuclear attack. The more prepared of the day – some might use the label, paranoid - dug up their lawns or vegetable gardens in order to construct bomb shelters in their own backyards.

But the vast majority of Americans didn't go underground to find safety. Instead they found solace and comfort by huddling in front of the electronic hearth in their own living rooms. America tuned in religiously to watch the westerns, detective shows, or anthologies that were on TV at the time. It was escapism at its best. And no television show provided this electronic port in storm better than the episodic family sitcom.

Former bandleader and radio performer Ozzie Nelson created one of the first TV family "sitcoms" with the introduction of *The Adventures of Ozzie and Harriet*. The show debuted on ABC in the fall of 1952, and was to become a template for the other family sitcoms – such as *Beaver* - that followed. Nelson's model of wholesome entertainment was meant to mirror the American way of life and to poke fun at its many foibles. Key to the success of these family programs was the inclusion of children in the plots, and it was here, on *The Adventures of Ozzie and Harriet,* that I got my first role on a network television series. It was just a bit part, like a lot of my roles back then, but it was still work, and I even got asked back to play on the show again a year later.

By 1955, I was starting to knock on the door of adolescence and puberty. I was transitioning out of the cute little kid role. My parts started becoming bigger, more demanding, and more frequent. This became the norm for my older brother Dayton as well. We were both getting lots of work, and Dayton still wasn't old enough to drive. This meant that my mom had become a full-time taxi driver for us. She'd drop Dayton off at Twentieth Century Fox to tape a TV episode, and then rush me off to another interview. The next week, I was at Universal and Dayton was at Republic. At times, it seemed as if the car never stopped running as it made circuits from one movie studio to the next all over Los Angeles and the Valley. We went through a lot of gas and my mom was constantly stopping at the Mobil station on Magnolia and Vineland to get a $1.25 worth of regular gas. Back then, a buck and a quarter would get you about 5 gallons.

Besides burning more fossil fuel than the average family, Dayton and my formal education didn't mirror the societal norm of the day either. With all of the TV and movie work that we were doing, we were out of school more than we were in it. But this still didn't mean that we got to skip any lessons. Each set we worked on would have a certified teacher that was required by law to give three hours of instruction per day in age-appropriate subjects. Most of the time, it was dedicated one on one instruction with a tutor, which is an incredible opportunity for learning. I regret to this day that I didn't take better advantage of it. I kind of goofed off a lot I guess. Oh well, I was the boy who would play Eddie Haskell some day, so maybe the shoe kind of fit.

After appearing on *The Adventures of Ozzie and Harriet*, I returned to the big screen in the 20th Century Fox production of *Good Morning Miss Dove*. Miss Dove was a 1955 tearjerker about a beloved small town schoolmarm who ends up terminally ill, only to see all of her students return to her deathbed as she passes. I played the young Tommy Baker; one of Miss Dove's students whom she soon discovers has a unique ability to work with his hands when she catches him repairing a broken watch. Always determined to have her students apply themselves and utilize their God-given talents, she encourages my character to do something big with his life. At the denouement of the film, the now grown up Dr. Thomas Baker (played by Robert Stack) returns as a successful surgeon to the bedside of the woman who changed his life.

A Scene from the 20th Century-Fox Production
"GOOD MORNING MISS DOVE"
In CinemaScope

With Jennifer Jones in "Good Morning Miss Dove." Copyright Twentieth Century Fox.

Although I never came close to going to medical school, the notion that I was good with my hands wasn't much of a stretch for me – even at a young age. Along with Dayton, I've always been very mechanically inclined. My pop was working all the time so he wasn't around very much. If Dayton or I wanted to build something, or fix something, we had to do it ourselves.

Dayton Osmond,
"When Ken was about nine or ten, he and I bought
an old Cushman motor scooter from a guy in Studio
City. I remember that it was just off of Laurel
Canyon and was next door to Natalie Wood's
house. We paid ten bucks for the scooter, and had
to push it all the way home to North Hollywood,
almost two miles. He and I rebuilt it and got it
running, 'running' being a relative term. Every time
you started it, the carburetor caught on fire. We just
learned to blow out the fire, and then we'd get on it
and ride around."

After *Miss Dove* and 20th Century, it was back over to
NBC Studios in Burbank for the TV anthology, *Matinee
Theatre*. Airing daily in the afternoons, it was essentially
filmed stage plays, broadcast live to the Los Angeles
area, and then transferred by Kinescope for distribution
to other markets. I played another small role that,
nonetheless, left a lasting impression on me.

The sets were the most God-awful color
combinations you could imagine; green walls, purple
carpet - everything was just a strange color! Even the
flowers on the table didn't look natural. They were fake
of course, but the colors were like no flowers I had ever
seen. Apparently, as a subsidiary of RCA, who was
working aggressively to promote color TVs as the new
standard, NBC had marching orders to really "pump up"
the volume of the color in their productions, even though
there were probably only two color TVs in Los Angeles
at the time.

After *Matinee Theatre*, I went on do some TV
westerns such as *Fury*, and *Annie Oakley*, along with
countless other anthologies and dramas. In 1957, I also
played on an episode of a short-lived series called *Circus
Boy*. It was the story of a young boy named *Corky,* who

was the orphaned son of circus performers who died while performing their act. The circus adopts Corky, and viewers followed his adventures as the show moved from town to town. Micky Dolenz, who would return to TV a decade later as one of *The Monkees*, played the lead character of Corky.

"Circus Boy" courtesy Sony Pictures Television. I played the character "Skinny." In front of me is Micky Dolenz.

By now Dayton and I each had over a decade of performing under our belts. Dayton was closing in on adulthood, and he was growing tired of the endless grind of hustling auditions and chasing parts. He pined for a steady paycheck and more regular hours. He began to work his way out of acting.

Unlike Dayton, I didn't want to throw in the towel on acting just yet and so in July of 1957, I went on an interview for a part in a new television series.

By now, Dayton was driving and he took me down to the interview that day. We drove in the 1950 Mercury that we had bought together for the outrageous sum of $215. It was a real jalopy, but we were proud of it for many reasons, not the least of which was the enterprising method in which we had earned the money to purchase it – by selling illegal fireworks we had smuggled home from our family trips back to Oklahoma.

We arrived at the interview, and I stepped out of the Mercury, thinking it was just going to be another one-off role I would do before it would be back to the grind of auditions all over again. I had no idea how wrong I was; this was the singular role that would define me, for good and for bad, for the rest of my life.

Eddie Haskell Trivia Answer Chapter 4
The 1/3 scale Mayflower ship model used in the
movie Plymouth Adventure is now prominently
displayed at Benjamin's Calabash Seafood
Restaurant in Myrtle Beach, South Carolina.

Eddie Haskell Trivia Chapter 5: Although Dayton
and Ken were very proud of their prized 1950
Mercury. They couldn't enjoy it for very long. Why?
Answer at the end of Chapter 6

SIX
EDDIE HASKELL

People often ask me where the character Eddie
Haskell comes from. I guess it's one of those enduring
mysteries of sitcoms, like, "Hey, how did the castaways
have all that stuff on *Gilligan's Island* if it was only
supposed to be a three-hour cruise?"

There are lots of theories. One of the ones I
remember hearing was that it was a navy buddy of one
of the show's writers, Connelly and Mosher. Another
story is that it was a friend of one of Connelly's sons.
Probably the most plausible and believable explanation
came from Bob Mosher III, son of the co-creator and
writer of the show, Bob Mosher Jr.

Bob Mosher III,
"His name was 'Buddy' Del Giorno, or at least
that's what we called him – I never knew his actual
first name. He was a real character, and my dad
had him figured out pretty well. He was always
overly polite and complimenting my mom on her
dress and so forth. But as soon as we got away from

the adults, he would be devising some trouble for us to get into. After the show had been on for a while, he realized that he was the inspiration for Eddie Haskell, and he was real proud of it; he wore it like a badge of honor."

With Bob Mosher III in his auto restoration shop.
It was Bob's friend "Buddy" Del Giorno that was most likely the
inspiration for Eddie Haskell.

I think in the end, Eddie could have been an amalgamation of people, because everybody knew an Eddie Haskell growing up, and every mother warned their child to stay away from him.

And just like there are lots of Eddies out in the world, there were a lot of wannabe Eddies in the casting room that day. I thought it was going to be a routine interview like all the rest, but when I got there, I saw that it was anything but. It was the cattle call to end all cattle calls. There were hundreds of kids there; some three years younger than me, some three years older; it was like every kid in town had showed up. All of us were there to try out for a part for a brand new TV show that we knew nothing about, much less, which character it was. To me it was just going to be one more bit part and a few extra bucks in my pocket.

Unbeknownst to the other child actors and to myself that day, the show had already been produced, but only as a pilot and under the title *It's A Small World*. It aired on April 23, 1957. The CBS network had picked it up as a series for the fall line-up with a, as yet to be determined, new title. The main characters had already been cast, but the search was on to replace an unpleasant character who had appeared as Frankie Bennett in the pilot. The incredibly talented performer and satirist, Harry Shearer, had played Frankie as a dark and mean-spirited kid who dupes Beaver (Jerry Mathers) and Wally (initially played by Paul Sullivan - more on that later) into thinking they could get a new bike by turning in milk bottle caps. It wasn't Shearer's first experience - or his last - playing underhanded characters.

Harry Shearer
I remember playing a similarly dark role in an episode of Ann Southern's sitcom Private Secretary, called The Little Caesar of Bleecker Street. My career has been built on doing that, to a certain extent (cf, C. Montgomery Burns, on The Simpsons, for example).

But Frankie was distant and aloof in his malevolence, not in the sneaking, conniving, "I'm your pal, Eddie" kind of way. I think that's what the show's producers were looking for to go forward with the series.

Eddie was going to be the smarmy, shifty neighborhood kid who was a consummate con artist and changeling. He could be completely unctuous to any adults he encountered, and then as soon as their backs were turned, he would morph into the nemesis for the other kids, as well as becoming a lightning rod and catalyst for any trouble he could stir up. Before long, Eddie Haskell would evolve from being merely a secondary character name, to a synonym for untrustworthy souls everywhere.

* * *

On the first day of the cattle call, I read for Harry Ackerman, who would later go on to develop the shows *Bewitched* and *I Dream of Jeannie*. A week after that first cattle call, I was called back for second audition and moved up the chain. By this point, the field of wannbe Eddies had been winnowed down to about thirty kids or so. I must have passed muster that day, because I was called back for a third time. This time, my competition for the part had narrowed down to only about four or five other kids.

The summer of 1957 was almost in the history books when my mother told me the good news – I had been selected to play the part of Edward Clark "Eddie" Haskell on the new TV series, *Leave It to Beaver*. The episode title was, *The New Neighbors*, and it was the fifth show of the first season. It would air six weeks later. I had several lines of dialogue to memorize, and I had a call time at Republic Studios in Studio City at 8:00 a.m. on September 23, 1957. The show would officially debut on Friday of the following week.

As always, I was happy to get work and to pad my resume, but to me and to everyone else at the time, including my mom, it was really no big thing. Part of the reason for this was that unlike the principal actors: Barbara Billingsley, Hugh Beaumont, Tony Dow, and Jerry Mathers, I didn't have a regular long-term contract. My agreement was like every other one I had had up to this point in time; I would have a one-time deal. The amazing thing is; even though I ended up being in 97 of the 235 episodes, I was never considered a season regular, and I never, ever had a long-term contract. Either way, as an actor, you never say, "no" to work, and instead respectfully channel the line from the movie *Animal House* and say, "Thank you sir, may I have another?"

Dayton again drove me down in the Mercury to my first day on the set. I guess you could say that it was a harbinger of good fortune that the car hadn't given up the ghost just yet and could still get me to the studio on time.

When I arrived, I was met by my "set mom", Iva Shaheen. Since my mom had become more involved working at Lola Moore's agency, she had less and less time to accompany me to my various jobs. Since I was still a juvenile, the law required that I be watched over by an adult who was legally responsible for me. My mom had hired Mrs. Shaheen to be my set mom, and she was really nice and ended up becoming one of my favorite people throughout my *Beaver* years. She made sure that I never got into (too much) trouble, and that I was where I was supposed to be when I needed to be there. She even accompanied me to the studio commissary during lunchtime and will go down in my personal Ken Osmond history as the person who taught me how to hold a fork properly to cut my meat. To this day, it's something that drives me crazy when I see people doing it the wrong way.

The script for episode 907A, *The New Neighbors,* had been dropped off by the studio at our house the previous Friday evening. In it, Eddie scares the Beaver into thinking the husband of the couple who had just moved in next door is going to kill him because his wife had kissed him. Wally initially doesn't want to be a part of the ruse played on his little brother, but Eddie throws his logic and high-pressure sales techniques into high gear and gets him to go along. *Heh, heh, heh!*

From this, my first ever scene on the show, the die was pretty much set that I was the conniving troublemaker your mom would forever tell you to avoid.

I was very good – at the time – with memorizing my lines, and only had to read the script twice through before having it committed to memory. Mrs. Shaheen directed me to the studio conference room where the script "table-read" was done every Monday morning. Inside the room that day were the writers and co-producers of the show, Bob Mosher Jr. and Joe Connelly, actors Barbara Billingsley, Hugh Beaumont, Tony Dow, Jerry Mathers, Phyllis Coates, and Charles Gray.

I would later learn that in a lot of ways, we were a mixed bag of entertainers. Besides being an experienced actor with a long list of credits, Hugh Beaumont was also an ordained Methodist minister and preached at a church in South Los Angeles. Barbara Billingsley was a former model, and had extensive stage and film experience. Jerry Mathers, who was nine years old at the time, was a lot like myself in that he started out acting at a very young age and had, like myself, performed in many small, uncredited parts in film.

Of everyone in the room that day, Tony Dow had the least industry experience, but the most interesting, serendipitous back story as to how he got into acting. A Junior Olympic Diving Champion, he was approached one day by a lifeguard at the pool where he trained. The lifeguard had aspirations of getting into acting, and wanted to audition for a part in a movie. The only problem was, the casting agency was looking for a father-son combo, and the lifeguard was unmarried. In short, he needed a "son" to accompany him on the interview and wanted to know if Tony would be interested. Not having anything to lose, Tony agreed. The irony was that his lifeguard "father" got turned down for the film, while Tony was asked to audition for another part.

That the role of Wally was even available to Tony was a fluke in itself. The child actor, Paul Sullivan had played Wally in the original pilot of the show *It's a Small World*. The producers were happy with Sullivan's portrayal as Beaver's older brother, but between the time of the pilot's airing, and when the series got picked up; Sullivan experienced a growth spurt. He towered over Jerry Mathers – and even Casey Adams, who played the original Ward Cleaver, that the producers felt no one would be convinced of his age. The hunt for a new Wally was on.

Also in the room with us that day was Norman Tokar, the director of this episode as well as many others. Norman was a former stage and radio actor who was best known for playing Henry Aldrich on the radio program *The Aldrich Family*. I didn't know it at the time, but Norman was to make a huge impact on my acting career, and had a big hand in helping me develop the Eddie character. He was a good director, and more importantly for a show such as Beaver that was *kid-centric*, he was very good at working with child actors.

The point of the table read was to have all of the actors in the same room read their lines aloud. The writers and director would sit in and take notes regarding any clumsy dialogue. Sometimes they would suggest a change on the spot and have the actor reread it, other times they would take notes for later rewrites.

After a couple of hours of read-through, we were excused. That evening, a revised script, called pink sheets, was dropped off at our house and I went through my lines again.

On Tuesday, we went to the set where we were going to film and we "blocked-in" our shots. Essentially, we would walk through the scene and check for any hiccups that could occur during the actual filming. If you were supposed to say this particular line and then walk over to the couch and sit down, then that's what you did. The stage was lit with simple stage lights, and besides the writers and director, only the wardrobe or prop person might be there to check for any problems. Other than that, there were no cameramen or lighting grips, or anyone else.

During this time in the industry, the child labor laws permitted children to work a maximum of only eight hours a day, *and that included three hours of school*. A lot of attention was paid by the producers to making sure that they utilized kids as efficiently as possible to avoid going over the time budget. For this reason, they usually liked to work us first and get any bugs ironed out, because they knew they could make the adults work overtime if they had to. By the end of the day Tuesday, we were given a shooting schedule for the rest of the week.

For *The New Neighbors* episode, I had three scenes to shoot for a total of six minutes or 25% of the show's run time of 24 minutes, which was pretty good for a new character's debut. By comparison, Frank Bank (Lumpy) had only about a minute of airtime on his debut of the show. We shot interiors in Wally and Beaver's room, interiors in the living room of the Cleaver house, and exteriors of the Cleaver house. It took all of the rest of the week to shoot.

On Friday afternoon we wrapped the episode and we were excused. No mention was made of me coming back to do another show and I said good-bye to my co-actors, thinking I wouldn't be back. I had no idea that I would spend the better part of a decade working with them, and that all of us would remain lifelong friends.

*Eddie Haskell Trivia Answer Chapter 5
Dayton and Ken's couldn't enjoy their 1950
Mercury very long because the engine seized after
only a couple of months. A removal of the oil pan
revealed that the boys had been ripped off: The
crankcase was filled with sawdust.*

*Eddie Haskell Trivia Chapter 6: If 'Buddy' Del
Giorno was in fact the true Eddie Haskell, he and
Ken Osmond were kindred spirits in what other
ways?
Answer at the end of Chapter 7*

SEVEN
SPUTNIK AND THE BEAVER

On October 4, 1957, two new radio signals began broadcasting to the United States. One of these signals was designed to intimidate and frighten, the other would serve to validate and reassure.

The Russian Sputnik satellite became the first man-made object to orbit the earth, and in the process, represented a giant leap ahead in what would become a decade long space race between the world's two superpowers.

Only 23 inches in diameter, Sputnik was technologically primitive by today's standards. The one important component it had onboard though was a radio transmitter that broadcast a constant "beep" on both the 20.005 and 40.002 MHz frequency. This was done purposely so that amateur radio hobbyists in the United States could monitor the signal and therefore not allow the United States government to deny the spacecraft's existence. I guess the Russians wanted to make sure they got credit for their achievement.

At the other end of the radio and ideological

spectrum, we began broadcasting as well that evening, with the debut episode of *Leave It to Beaver* entitled, *Beaver Gets Spelled.*

The episode was written and produced by Joe Connelly and Bob Mosher, the same duo who had produced the pilot. Like many TV writers of the day, Connelly and Mosher had come from writing radio. They were best known for the *Amos and Andy* radio program, which they transitioned with when it moved to television in 1951.

Both men were married and had children, (Connelly had seven, Mosher had two) and so with *Leave It to Beaver*, they wanted to create a more "kid-centric" type of TV sitcom. Up until this point, all of the other family shows had focused on the travails of the parents in raising their children, not necessarily on the experiences and emotions of the children themselves. Even the name *Leave It to Beaver*, hinted at a younger focus compared to other shows of the time. With their adult titles, *Ozzie and Harriet, Father Knows Best, Make Room for Daddy*, and later, *The Donna Reed Show*, the other family sitcoms of the day all suggested more of an emphasis on the parents in the show.

One of the bizarre things about our show's premiere on Oct 4, 1957 was that the scheduled debut episode was not shown, and a substitute episode had to be used instead. The reason for this was the long arm of the network censors. That's right, even innocent little Beaver fell victim to the moral watchdogs of the time.

The show originally set to air that night, was *Captain Jack*. In it, Wally and the Beaver secretly mail order a baby alligator through a comic book ad. When the little critter arrives, they soon learn that he has to stay damp in order to survive. The only place they can think to keep him is in the toilet tank in their bathroom. Believe it or not, the censors felt that it would be too racy to show an actual toilet on TV!

The debate went back and forth until finally the censors' acquiesced and allowed the toilet to be shown – but only from the tank up. After all the squabbles, *Captain Jack* became the second episode of *Leave It to Beaver* to air.

It's hard to believe, that with the all the junk that's on TV today, and what they get away with saying or doing, that a toilet could be considered too racy. Like I said before, "I loved growing up when I did in the '50s."

Connelly and Mosher hit the mark with the debut show as it received warm praise from the critics for its candor and charm of the world as seen through a child's eyes. I honestly don't remember watching the first show – or even my debut episode, *The New Neighbors* when it aired a little less than a month later on November 1. Connelly and Mosher had told Jerry and Tony that they didn't want them to watch their own shows for fear they might become too critical of themselves and try to modify the way they portrayed their characters.

As I wasn't on long-term contract for my work, I was exempted from this restriction. My lack of interest in watching myself perform on the small screen might have come from a more primal urge. I was in junior high school now, North Hollywood Junior High to be exact, and my interests generally ran toward only two things: cars and girls.

The 1950 Mercury had gasped its last breath by now, and Dayton and I once again pooled our money to buy another set of wheels. Our next car was a 1952 Ford and it was a far better car and more reliable than the Merc had been. This was fortuitous, as I needed dependable transportation to have Dayton drive me around in, especially when I was squiring girls.

I had several "girlfriends" in junior high school, but no one serious. And I didn't attract them because I was a "movie star." Like I said before, it was a different era back then, and being a kid actor was no big thing. Our "dates" mostly consisted of cutting school and going to the beach.

My real date was with destiny, and it came on October 17, 1957 just a little less than two weeks after *Leave It to Beaver* premiered and before my first episode had even aired; Republic Studios called – they wanted me back for another episode.

* * *

In my second episode, *The Clubhouse*, Eddie once again is picking on the Beaver when he hijacks his idea to form a boys club. Eddie turns the tables on Beaver by jacking up the initiation dues in order to exclude him. It was a pretty weak show by anyone's standards, but it did help in the further development of the Eddie character and reinforced the fact that Eddie didn't care much for the Beaver. Either way, it was another credit, and up until this point in my career I had only been on the same show twice – *Ozzie and Harriet* – and on those I was essentially an extra. With solid dialogue and lots of camera time, *Leave It to Beaver* was slowly molding me into the Eddie icon.

By my third show, I was beginning to wonder if something might really come of this. The episode was *Voodoo Magic*. In it, Eddie convinces Wally and Beaver to go see a movie about voodoo, after their mother has strictly forbidden it. Eventually, June Cleaver finds out about their disobedience and the boys are punished. So angry is Beaver at Eddie Haskell, that he makes an Eddie "voodoo doll" and sticks pins into it. But the next day at school, when he and Wally hear that Eddie is sick, Beaver becomes worried that he put a real whammy on Eddie. It was a fun show to make, I had a lot of lines, and I got to show off my Eddie talents for feinting illness. *Heh, heh, heh!*

With Tony Dow on the set of Leave It to Beaver. You can just imagine Eddie trying to con Wally into some mischief. Courtesy of Universal Studios Licensing LLC.

Part of the fun of doing *Leave It to Beaver* was the fact that there were other kids around, and that Connelly and Mosher made sure we had fun when we weren't in school or doing scenes. Just outside the sound stage, they set up a basketball hoop for us to play with, and when we were on the back lot, we would play baseball in a large open field. In a way, it was a lot like being a regular kid: school, play, and a little work. It may have seemed an odd way to grow up, but again, I had never known any different. Occasionally, our lives during the downtime on the set really imitated the art we were portraying.

> *Tony Dow,*
> *"I remember one time we were playing baseball and someone hitting a long fly ball. Steve McQueen used to park his Jaguar next to the sound stage where he was working, and the ball hit his windshield and shattered it. Being just like normal kids, we all took off and got the hell out of there. Eventually we went back though and left a note on his windshield. Steve was real nice about it and just laughed it off."*

…and sometimes, I inadvertently created some real authentic Eddie moments all on my own. *Heh, heh, heh!*

> *Tony Dow,*
> *"One day when we were all in school on the set, Kenny brought in some very provocative pictures. And Frank, Ken, and I were all 'oohing' and 'aahing' about them. I don't know what happened, but I ended up getting caught with them and taking the brunt for it. So Ken had a bit of the Eddie side to him in real life."*

By the end of the show's first year, I had racked up fourteen appearances. In them, Eddie Haskell began to really establish himself as a character. He was Eddie the con man, Eddie the whiner, Eddie the braggart, and even Eddie the consultant when I become the go-to person for Wally and Beaver when they needed to cover up breaking the window in their dad's car. Even when I wasn't appearing on the show, the name Eddie Haskell would often be referenced.

The director, Norman Tokar really worked with me on the character traits, including the famous *Heh, heh, heh!* "Eddie cackle." It became a trademark of the Eddie character.

It was a great time and I was so glad to be working. I wrapped my final episode of the first season on June 12, 1958, a couple of days after I turned fifteen years old. We had been informed several weeks earlier that we had been renewed for a second season, so it was like an early birthday present for me. Sputnik may have been launched on the same day as *Leave It to Beaver*, but it fell back to earth in just a couple of months and burnt up in the atmosphere. Over a half century later, *Beaver* is still broadcasting somewhere in the world. The show has been translated into Spanish, Japanese, and even Swahili.

An even more memorable present came to me when a secretary from the production company tracked me down on the set and handed me an envelope; after a decade of acting on the big and small screen, I had finally received my first fan mail.

Eddie Haskell Trivia Answer Chapter 6
Both Ken, and the inspiration for the Eddie
character, Buddy Del Giorno, were "Valley" boys,
Ken from North Hollywood, Buddy from Sherman
Oaks, only a few miles away. Both also shared a
love of motorcycles, and they were very close in
age; Buddy being younger by only one year.

Eddie Haskell Trivia Chapter 7: Although Sputnik
and Beaver both launched on Oct 4, 1957, what
other significant event took place - just the day

before?
Answer at the end of Chapter 8

EIGHT
"DEAR MR. OSMAND..."

I honestly can't remember what that first fan letter said, and unfortunately, I never held onto it. I always responded to them though, because that's what my mom and pop always taught me. I'm sure the fan wrote about how much they loved the show, and how great an actor they thought I was. But then they would always qualify the statement by saying that they *really* didn't like the character Eddie Haskell, because he was just so mean and sneaky.

Sometimes, I would get an irate letter, blasting me for being such a rotten, cowardly person. Tony would occasionally receive them as well, the writer lambasting him for letting Eddie do all that bad stuff to the Beaver. And why couldn't he just punch that Eddie Haskell in the nose some time?

To some people, I guess all TV is "reality" TV.

I didn't receive the bulk of the fan mail on the show. That honor was reserved for Jerry and Tony; Jerry because he was just so darn cute, and Wally, well because he was just so darn cute too...but in a little more grownup way.

After the first season of the show, Tony became an heartthrob and was featured in all the teen magazines of the day. Sometimes, Frank Bank (Lumpy) and I would get a hold of a magazine, and bring it to the set and tease him about it.

We went on hiatus for the show in mid-June and didn't have to report back until the second week of August. One of the other things that Connelly and Mosher were good about, was making sure we all had our summer vacations to enjoy as kids. My summer was spent doing what other kids mostly did during the summer in Southern California: going to the beach, chasing girls, and cruising around with Dayton in our Ford. I had less than a year before I got my driver's license, and I was itching to get behind the wheel and be able to legally drive. Notice that I used the word *legally* here. Like most kids, Dayton and I would push the limits of the law sometimes. He was the one who taught me to drive, and let's just say, you could have given me my driver's test when I was fourteen, and I could have probably passed it with flying colors.

* * *

By the end of *Leave It to Beaver's* first season, the US had gained a little on the Soviets by launching the American satellite, Explorer I in January of 1958. But the space race was far from over, and the cold war still loomed like a dark cloud over the horizon. Without any of us realizing it at the time, *Leave It to Beaver* offered an oasis and a safe harbor for those wanting to forget the evils and the frightening realities of the world at the time. The town of Mayfield and the Cleaver family might have been idealized, but the show represented all that was good and pure about America – and America needed to be reminded about that right then.

Besides the didactic lessons that were craftily woven into the stories, the cast and the crew maintained a high standard of conduct as well. We were professionals, plain and simple. Nobody was a "star" and there were no set "divas."

But if there was a set "enforcer" back then, it would have been Hugh Beaumont. If any of us kids would get silly, or start laughing a little too much about somebody blowing their line or whatever, Hugh was usually the one to bring us back around. Mind you he wasn't mean, but he was stern, in the way any good father figure would be.

One of the amazing things about Hugh was that although he played an average middle-class father and husband on the show, most of his work before coming to *Beaver* had been playing tough guys in gangster movies, or as the private investigator Michael Shayne.

* * *

We arrived back after our hiatus in early August 1958 ready to roll up our sleeves and get back to work. There were some changes that were coming however.

For one thing, our time slot had been moved again. Originally, the show was on Fridays at 7:30 p.m. Then, midway through the first season, CBS decided to move it to Wednesday at 8:00 p.m. as part of a jockeying effort to play opposite the shows they thought they could do better against, such as *Wagon Train*. Ironically, I would actually do an episode of *Wagon Train* that same year, but I wouldn't be broadcast against my own show.

The change that season had us moving once again. This time, we were shuffled to Thursdays at 7:30 p.m. and more importantly, we were being moved from CBS to ABC. The move to a different network was more about sponsorship deals than anything else. As long as their checks cashed, I didn't really care.

Another big change had less to do with business, and more about child psychology. In addition to wanting to create a show that saw the world through a child's eyes, Connelly and Mosher also wanted us to maintain *our* innocence – especially the younger kids. Being parents themselves, they saw firsthand the influence that older kids could have on younger ones. To this end, they began separating us as best they could. From the second season and beyond, the big kids; Wally, Lumpy, Tooey, and I were put in separate classrooms from the younger children; Jerry, Larry, and Gilbert. They also tried to stagger our shooting times as best as possible.

> *Jerry Mathers,*
> *"We were totally segregated. Tony and Ken had their own teacher, I had my own teacher. And when I wasn't working with the older boys, I didn't really spend much time with them."*

One big welcome change – at least as far as I was concerned - was that to my amazement and delight, the very first show we would film that second season would feature me in the episode's title role, *Eddie's Girl*. In the story, Eddie introduces Wally to a girl that he's claiming to be "his girl." She ends up liking Wally instead, and asking him to a dance. When Eddie find out, he's upset and hurt, but then realizes he can't make people like him. In the end, Eddie fakes being sick and asks Wally to take her to the dance for him.

Tony Dow, Karen Green, Ken Osmond - Leave It To Beaver "Eddie's Girl"
Airing Thursday Oct. 9, 1958 7:30 - 8:00PM PST
Courtesy of Universal Studios Licensing LLC.

I liked doing the episode for several reasons. One, I had more airtime and lines than I had ever had as an actor, and two, for the very first time I got to portray a vulnerable and more sympathetic Eddie character. Any sympathy garnered for Eddie from this episode didn't last for long though.

Beaver and Chuey was groundbreaking for the show, and for television in general at the time, by showing tolerance and compassion for immigrants. At least everybody in the show showed tolerance, except for good old Edward Clark Haskell. In the episode, Eddie tricks Beaver into insulting a young immigrant friend of his by telling him to say, "Usted tiene una cara como puerco," which translates to, "You have a face like a pig." Of course, the young boy is crushed, everyone is bewildered by this bizarre turn of international relations, and Eddie has once again upset the apple cart and left a debris field of emotions in his wake. Maybe Wally *should* punch Eddie. *Heh, heh, heh!*

I did only three more episodes that second season and was excused by September 3, 1958 after wrapping the episode *Wally's Present,* which stayed in the can until after the New Year when it was broadcast.

Besides having less work on the show that season, and our imposed segregation from the younger actors, the year brought many other changes, both on and off the set.

By now my brother Dayton had fully divorced himself from acting. This didn't mean, however, that he was out of the entertainment industry. He followed in Pop's footsteps and became a prop maker and set-builder for the studios as well. The fact that he had moved on at about the same time that I had become a recurring character on *Leave It to Beaver* helped to never cause any animosity between Dayton and myself. He was happy for my success, and in fact, even felt like he might have gotten the better end of the deal.

> *Dayton Osmond,*
> *"I thought it was funny that Ken was making all this big money when he was working, but he only worked a couple of days a month. By comparison, I was working five or six days a week at the studios, and at the end of the month, I had more money in my pocket."*

The other thing that changed for me on the set that year, was that I was getting closer to Frank Bank. We had worked briefly together on one episode, *Tenting Tonight*, during the first season, and now we worked again on the episode *The Shave*.

Frank was the oldest of the child actors on the show, and was the only one who had a driver's license, which was something I really coveted. Frank also was a larger-than-life guy who drove hot cars, which I was very much into at the time.

During the downtime on the set, when Tony and the others would be playing sports, Frank and I would sit around and talk about cars, girls, and even money. Frank's dad had a very successful butcher shop, and Frank was always intrigued with making money, something else that sparked my fancy. He would later go on to become a very successful bond trader and eventually managed some of my money, along with that of many other celebrities, including some from *Leave It to Beaver* such as Barbara Billingsley.

On June 7, 1959 I turned 16 years old, a milestone day in many a young boy's life. Unfortunately for me, it was a Sunday, and the local Department of Motor Vehicle office in North Hollywood was closed. But the very next day, I was there bright and early with my mom as the front doors opened. I was the first one in line and the first one to take a test that day. Dayton was working and had our 1952 Ford, so I had to take my test in my mom's 1953 Buick. Having driven the Ford more often, I was more familiar with it and would have liked to have taken my test in it. But I had driven all sorts of vehicles, both on and off the road through the years, and I knew I could handle just about anything.

I passed my test the first go-round and was now added to the ranks of teenage terrors on the Los Angeles streets. I would no longer have to be driven to the studio on the days we filmed *Leave It to Beaver*. In fact, I would be picking up my set mom, Iva Shaheen, at her house in Burbank, on my way in to the studio. I always thought it ironic that in the eyes of the state, I could be trusted with a two-ton hunk of metal on the highway, but I couldn't be trusted to watch over myself on the set. Don't try to make sense of the government, you'll only hurt yourself.

One more very significant change occurred during the year of that second season of *Leave It to Beaver*. In fact, it was a change that would alter my commute with Mrs. Shaheen when I picked her up on my way in to film episodes. We would be taking a different route in to work; *Leave It to Beaver* had moved.

> *Eddie Haskell Trivia Answer Chapter 7*
> *The significant event that took place, only one day before the launch of both Sputnik and Beaver, was the birth of Christopher J. Lynch. Ken Osmond claims the co-author of his biography wanted to make sure he didn't miss the first episode of Beaver. Heh, heh, heh!*

> *Eddie Haskell Trivia Chapter 8: Ken Osmond still receives a large amount of fan mail to this day. A big percentage of it comes from where?*
> *Answer at end of Chapter 9*

NINE
UNIVERSAL STUDIOS

The move from Republic Studios had been predicated by the fact that the show's sponsors could get a better deal at Universal Studios, and it had been planned out well in advance. Not wanting to have the Cleavers abruptly show up in another home without explanation, Connelly and Mosher began weaving harbingers of the coming move into the story lines toward the end of season two, beginning with an episode titled *Beaver Says Good-bye*. I wasn't in the episode, but it's very cute and has Beaver, after hearing June and Ward inform him they've made an offer on a new house, telling his classmates that he's moving. As a result, Beaver's classmates buy him all kinds of going-away presents but, as you can imagine, the deal falls through and he has to give them all back.

We did make the move in season three, and it was to be our home for the rest of the series' run. We had a new sound stage, Stage 17, and the Cleavers had a new home at 211 Pine Street, on what is known as Colonial Street on the Universal back lot. It's a street with lots of movie and TV show history. The new Cleaver house – now sans the ubiquitously white picket fence from the Republic Studios house at 485 Maple Drive – was originally known as the "Paramount House" from the 1955 film *The Desperate Hours*. In later years, it would become the home of *Marcus Welby, M.D.* Just across the street from that home was the house used in the TV series *Bachelor Father* starring John Forsythe, as well as the "House of Seven Gables" from the 1940 movie of the same name.

Probably their most famous neighbor was just a stone's throw – or a Wally Cleaver football throw - from the Cleaver home. "The Maxim House" from the 1946 movie, *So Goes My Love*, would later be transformed into "The Munster House" when that series premiered in 1964. The Victorian style home was even featured in several *Beaver* episodes. Little did I realize when we were shooting there at the time, that I would be doing an episode on *The Munsters* in just a couple of years, and that I would once again be working for Connelly and Mosher.

And speaking of working, after a long career with Lola Moore, my mom had decided to strike out on her own. She opened The Pearl Agency and had an office on La Brea Avenue between Hollywood Boulevard and Sunset Boulevard She never represented Dayton or myself, and instead was focused on trying to build up a completely different stable of talent.

Even with *Leave It to Beaver's* move to Universal, we still followed the same rigid format as we did during the Republic years. We still did table reads on Monday, shot blocking on Tuesday, and filming the rest of the week. The filming was also still done with a single camera, a 35mm Mitchell, the same type used in movie production. Shooting single camera costs more and extends the shooting times. By comparison, a modern sitcom is shot with three cameras and only requires one day to shoot. Our costs per episode back then were around $45k, a considerable amount. But when you amortize that amount over a half-century of continual syndication income, it's a bargain.

One of my favorite shows I did that year was *Wally's Test*. In it, Wally, Lumpy, and Eddie have a big history test coming up in school. Eddie, of course, has a plan to hide the answers in the towel dispenser in the boy's bathroom so that he and Lumpy can pass with flying colors. But Wally takes the high road and buckles down to study. I liked doing this episode for several reasons. One, I had lots of lines and airtime. And two, it had Tony, Lumpy, and Eddie working very closely together. The show's title may have been *Leave It to Beaver* but this was the Wally, Lumpy, and Eddie episode all the way. *Heh, heh, heh!*

Off camera, we were getting closer as well.

One of the fun things we did was to play practical jokes on our wardrobe man, Hughie McFarland. He was a real nice guy, but very gullible. You could pull a joke on him on Wednesday, and then on Thursday repeat the same exact prank. It was basically silly kid's stuff: switching wardrobe with another actor, hiding things, but we had lots of fun and everyone loved Hughie.

The real *teenage* fun started when we got to go off the set – for lunchtime.

Bob's Big Boy Restaurant was located at Riverside and Pass Avenues in nearby Toluca Lake. It was an iconic spot that has since become a *State Point of Historical Interest* by the State of California. Way back then, it even had car-hop service. And while many neophyte actors and stagehands would be thrilled to eat in the Universal commissary in the hopes of spotting some, as teenage boys, we were much more interested in spying something else entirely – girls. *Heh, heh, heh!*

Even though we worked at Universal, Bob's was located close to the Warner Brothers' lot, and during lunchtime, a lot of the Warner secretaries used to eat there. I remember many a day when we would pile into Frank's latest hot set of wheels and charge on over there at lunchtime. On the days when we acquiesced and let Jerry come along with us – remember, we were still teenage boys and he was a little kid – we would have him sit in the backseat.

Sometimes, Tony would opt to ride over with his stand-in, a man named Pat Curtis. Pat had a beautiful Corvette convertible, and in addition to having the hot car, would later go on to marry one of Hollywood's hottest women: Raquel Welch. Wow, a Corvette and Raquel Welch; Frank Bank could only dream.

Of course, this interesting bit of trivia regarding Tony's stand-in's future love interest, morphed legs a few years later and became a rumor that it was in fact, *Tony Dow* who had gone on to marry Raquel Welch. This was to be one of the many wild rumors that grew out of the show concerning Tony, Jerry, and even Barbara. Of course, the most outrageous and salacious of these urban legends would be subscribed to me.

By the end of season three, I had done another sixteen episodes, my personal record on a show to this point. One of these is the show that is typically cited as one of Eddie's signature episodes, *The Hypnotist*. In it, Eddie dupes the Beaver into thinking that he has hypnotized him and cannot break the spell. Wally comes to Beaver's rescue again and ends up exposing Eddie as faking it. The episode ends with Wally chasing Eddie down the street until he falls into a mud puddle. *Heh, heh, heh!*

There were also several more episodes that prominently featured Wally, Lumpy, and myself. In *Wally's Election,* Eddie nominates Wally to run against

Lumpy in the campaign for class president.

But the most important statistic that season came for the show itself. This happened February 22, 1960 about halfway through the season. We hit the magic 100 episode mark, a number that is considered a gold standard for TV shows, and one that just about guarantees syndication after the show has ended.

Taking care of the hand that feeds you; myself and several other actors at Lola Moore's birthday party. My mom played host for the affair.

Since we were all now comfortably ensconced in our new digs on the Universal lot, season four seemed a lot like an extension of season three. During that season, I worked on nineteen episodes, or more than half of those filmed that year. This season also featured another full "Eddie" title with the episode *Eddie's Double-Cross.* Like the previous episode, *Eddie's Girl,* this showed a very human and vulnerable side to Eddie that I loved playing.

Good times. Mom, Pop, Dayton and myself pose for a family portrait.

Season four also had one of the most defining of all of the Beaver episodes, and the one that many people consider their all time favorite, *In The Soup*. In it, Beaver is goaded – amazingly not by Eddie this time, but by his friend Whitey - to prove that there's no soup inside a giant cup on a billboard. Naturally, Beaver falls in and becomes trapped. Hours later, he's rescued by the fire department, and humiliated in front of a large crowd of gawking spectators – one of whom is the wisecracking heckler, Eddie Haskell. *Heh, heh, heh!*

Sitting around the table on Monday morning to do our reads of the script for *In The Soup*, all of us kids were sitting a bit higher in our chairs that fourth season. There was a very important reason for this, and it had nothing to do with us suddenly learning good posture. It was because we were all growing up. Jerry was now twelve years old and almost a teenager, Tony had just turned sixteen and had gotten his driver's license, and Frank Bank was now nineteen.

To Barbara Billingsley, who was only five-foot-five, this meant a switch to high heels in order to keep us from towering over her. To me, my advancing years meant something far more ominous; I was less than a year away from turning eighteen, and this meant I would soon be eligible for the draft.

> *Eddie Haskell Trivia Answer Chapter 8*
> *A large amount of Ken Osmond's fan mail comes from prison. It seems that Eddie Haskell is a very popular fellow with those who are behind bars. Go figure.*
>
> *Eddie Haskell Trivia Chapter 9: In a moment of serendipity, Ken Osmond, along with Tony Dow and Jerry Mathers, had an occasion to drive by his mom's talent agency offices in 2013. What was the*

special occasion?
Answer at end of Chapter 10

TEN
FORT ORD

Monterey, California

Even though the Korean Conflict was considered over in 1953, it had ended in what could only be described as a stalemate, and proxy wars were still being waged by the communists on numerous fronts around the world. In 1956, Russia and China had moved into the country of Vietnam, a part of the world that had previously been known as French Indochina. And just a year prior, in 1959, a determined Fidel Castro had overthrown Cuba's president and a faithful American ally, Fulgencio Batista. In short, the communists were rapidly surrounding America, and the US was not going to take it lying down.

I was ready, willing, and able to serve my country, but like many other young men at the time, I wanted to have some control over how I served. Between juggling high school, and acting in even more *Leave It to Beaver* episodes than I ever had before, I began to explore my options.

It didn't take much consideration before I settled on the army reserves as my poison of choice. Dayton had enlisted three years prior, and had enjoyed a relatively benign experience. I would still have to go through regular army basic training, but my time commitment would be less than with the regular army, and I hoped this would allow me to continue acting. By this point, *Leave It to Beaver* had been on for four seasons and its popularity didn't show any signs of abating soon. I wanted to ride this wave as long as I could.

I enlisted in the army reserves in the spring of 1961 when I was still seventeen years old. My start date would be deferred until after high school graduation which meant that I could still finish my education at North Hollywood High School. In the meantime, I continued to work and to prepare for my last days as a high school senior: I went to the senior prom with a girl named Donna, finished up my classes, and started to prepare for graduation. What I wasn't prepared for, was what came next.

Like most high schools, there was a day toward the end of the school year that was unofficially designated as senior "cut day" when everybody cut out of school and went to the beach or whatever. The school's Vice Principal had come out a few weeks prior with an edict that if you did not come to school on that day, you would not be included in the graduation.

Well as it turned out, I was working on *Leave It to Beaver* that day and I wasn't in school. I had the signed slip from the set tutor, and so the school would still get their money, which was what they were worried about. And so the day of the graduation, which was about two weeks after I turned eighteen, I showed up in my cap and gown ready to graduate with my classmates. There was a line of students, girl/boy, white/blue, going up into the bleachers. I approached one of the school administrators and told her that I hadn't been there on the rehearsal day, and didn't know where to go. She looked at me and said, "Well if you weren't here that day, then you can't graduate."

And I stared back at her and said, "The hell I'm not,' and I stormed off.

I found the last girl in line and got in right behind her, and they never kicked me out because of it. *Heh, heh, heh!*

* * *

On July 9, 1961 my family dropped me off at the bus station in downtown Los Angeles. I had already said good-bye to my girlfriend, Sharon a few hours earlier, and promised to write her as much as I could. I said one last good-bye to my family and climbed onto the bus with my fellow recruits for the long, quiet ride up to the Central California Coast, three hundred fifty miles away. It was the first time in my life I had ever been away from home by myself, and like every other kid on the ride up there, I was scared.

We arrived at Fort Ord nine long hours later and were immediately put through the processing mill: haircut, medical checkout, uniform issue, and a host of other tasks. It was an assembly line designed to break you down before you were built up again in the army's mold. In just a couple of hours I went from being Ken Osmond, child actor and the man who had made Eddie Haskell a household name, to a shaved-head, OD green fatigued, Recruit Osmond. Like everyone else there that day, I was nothing, and the US army would make sure over the next couple of months that I knew it.

Just one more terrified and confused Army recruit.

Even the fact that I was an actor meant nothing special here, as Fort Ord had seen its share of entertainers pass through: David Janssen had done his hitch here, along with Martin Milner, and even Clint Eastwood had spent a year here as an army lifeguard.

One of most comical aspects of basic training for me was shaving my beard - because I didn't have one! Even so, they still make you "shave" every morning. One morning, right after I had first gotten there, we fell out for company formation. A drill sergeant came up to me and screamed,

"DID YOU SHAVE THIS MORNING RECRUIT OSMOND?"

Being so green and dumb, I answered honestly, "NO SERGEANT!"

"WELL THEN GET BACK IN THERE AND SHAVE!" he screamed back.

So I went back into the barracks, pulled an Eddie Haskell, and just stood around the latrine for about five minutes doing nothing. Then I came back out and rejoined the ranks.

The drilled sergeant stomped right over to me and said, "THAT'S BETTER RECRUIT. DON'T LET IT HAPPEN AGAIN."

"YES SERGEANT!"

There's the right way, the wrong way, the military way…and the Eddie Haskell way. *Heh, heh, heh!*

Even though basic training wasn't so tough for me physically – the LAPD was much tougher – it was still a very lonely time and I missed my family greatly. I remember walking fire watch in barracks one night. Everyone else was asleep and I was all by myself with lots of time to think. I went out on the fire escape and looked out into the blackness of the night and thought, like a million other grunts had before me, "What the hell am I doing here?"

And like a million other recruits before me, I made it through. I graduated from basic training in September of 1961 and had the requisite thirty days of leave. My time off wouldn't be spent drinking or carousing though, as I had a job to go back to. The fifth season of *Leave It to Beaver* was upon us and we had some shows to film.

Connelly and Mosher knew my situation and were able to shuffle the schedule so that I could get in some episodes before I had to report back to Fort Ord. We did three episodes before I had to return: *Wally's Car,*

Wally's Weekend Job, and *Wally's Big Date.* If you look closely you'll notice, my hair is shorter in those episodes and the stylist had to really work some magic to make it look somewhat reasonable.

My Army graduation picture.

Besides the shorter hair, the fact that I was an adult and had graduated high school meant that I no longer had to attend classes, and I no longer had to have a set mom. It was nice to be liberated, but I'll always remember Mrs. Iva Shaheen fondly.

We had barely wrapped the third show on Friday when I had to drive right back up to Fort Ord. It was here where I began my Military Operational Specialty or MOS which was my job as a small arms repairman. In layman's terms, I was a gunsmith, although most gunsmiths don't generally work on machine guns. Most also don't have the backlog of work that we did. The shop I worked out of had row after row of racks of weapons: M-1 Garands, M-1 Carbines, and BARs, all needing to be repaired. Some just had broken firing pins, but some were just plain worn out from so many rounds being put through them. You'd fix one, and then there would be hundreds more lined up to be fixed.

It seemed like it would never let up, until one day, while I was busy repairing a .30 caliber machine gun I heard, "Private Osmond?"

I turned toward the voice.

"Yes Sergeant," I said smartly.

"Are you the same man who plays Eddie Haskell on the show *Leave It to Beaver*?

"Yes Sergeant."

"How would you like to do me a favor and do some personal appearances? I think if you can help me out, I can arrange it to get you back down to Los Angeles to do some more shows."

"I'd love to Sergeant."

* * *

His name was Les Judson. He was a World War II vet and was the Master Sergeant at Fort Ord responsible for Special Services. For those not in the military, Special Services handled all matter of entertainment in the military, utilizing their own talented personnel, as well as civilians. Here again, I was in esteemed company with some of the other entertainers who had come before me: Ken Berry, Sammy Davis, Jr. and Frank Gorshin. Obviously, I wouldn't have the name recognition of the most famous of all entertainers to don a set of fatigues, as Elvis Presley had been discharged just a year prior, but I got the impression that Judson still considered me quite a prize.

The quid pro quo came down to this: I would go out with Master Sergeant Judson to do personal appearances. These were mostly either on the base or in the local area, and I would be introduced as Eddie Haskell, talk a little bit, shake hands, and sign autographs. They were pretty much "meet and greet" type of affairs that I could do in my sleep, and they sure as heck beat tearing down M-1 Garands all day!

For Judson's part, he would get me passes that would allow me to go home to Los Angeles and film more episodes. And so that's what I did for the next two years.

* * *

Back on the show, I found myself being featured more prominently in episodes along with Tony and Frank. Besides the periodic focus on the older boys' lives, the relationship of Eddie with the younger actors on the show was also changing. Jerry was getting older now – and bigger. His voice had deepened and he no longer suffered under Eddie's incessant bullying. In short, the Beaver wasn't going to take any more guff off of Eddie.

Jerry Mathers,
"I think this all came about because the show's
producers were starting to get lots of letters from

fans saying they were tired of Beaver getting picked on by Eddie, and that he should start standing up to him."

I ended up doing sixteen episodes that year, not a record for me, but still quite a lot considering how much they needed to work around my schedule. My mother helped to coordinate all of this with the show's producers and did a great job of juggling things. By the end of this season though, all of that would abruptly end.

We were close to wrapping the final episode of the season, and I was just two days away from my nineteenth birthday, when I received an urgent phone call. My mother had just been in a horrific car accident.

Eddie Haskell Trivia Answer Chapter 9
Jerry, Tony, and Ken were riding together in the 2013 Hollywood Christmas Parade when their car had to be rerouted. They drove right past the location of The Pearl Agency on La Brea.

Eddie Haskell Trivia Chapter 10: In 1962, while filming the fifth season of Leave It to Beaver, Ken Osmond escorted his girlfriend Charla, to the Academy Awards ceremony. Not able to compete with the limousines of all of the stars that night, how did he still manage to squire his date to the awards in style that magical evening?
Answer at end of Chapter 11

ELEVEN
JUNE 5,1962

My mom had been heading west on the Ventura Freeway, also called US 101, when tragedy struck. It was a single car accident, no other cars impacted her, and the weather was clear. The Renault she was driving had a complete failure of the steering mechanism. Essentially, my mom lost all control of her car. The Renault veered toward the edge of the freeway, broke through the guardrail, and went sailing off into space. The car hit and rolled, and in the process, she was ejected from it; like most vehicles of the time, it was not equipped with seatbelts.

Mom was alive when they got her to the hospital, though not in the best condition. In addition to cuts and bruises, she was unable to move. The doctors feared the worst and drilled holes into her skull to insert pins. She remained in traction in the hospital for several months until it was determined that she could leave. But she wouldn't be walking out of the hospital under her own power; she was paralyzed from the neck down, and would remain this way for the rest of her life.

Because of Pop's connection with the film industry through his union, my mother was transported to the Motion Picture & Television Country House and Hospital in nearby Woodland Hills. Founded in 1940 as the Motion Picture Country House, the acute care hospital was added to the property in 1948. Scores of old time actors, and others from the industry, spent the final years of their life there.

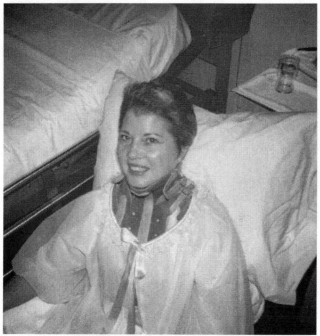

No matter what the circumstances, my mom Pearl always maintained a positive attitude.

Although my mom spent a good deal of her time there, she would come home on occasion for extended visits, and that meant things had to change around the house. Pop, Dayton, and I worked to modify it by widening the doorways to accommodate her wheelchair, putting in a hospital bed, and even installing a hydraulic hoist to get her in and out of bed.

Mom's injury hit all of us like a ton of bricks. Here she was, the sparkplug and the workhorse of our family, and she was incapacitated, down for the count. But mom was never a complainer, and she wanted us to go on as if nothing had changed. Mostly, she wanted us each to get back to work, and so that's what I did.

* * *

Season six of *Leave It to Beaver* had me working on more episodes than I ever had before. I would do a total of twenty-five out of the thirty-nine that we filmed that year. Jerry had grown even taller over the summer, and now stood nearly eye to eye with me. He was now fourteen years old, as old as I was when I started on the show six seasons prior. We were all growing up, and it changed the focus of the episodes, as well as the dynamic between us. There were no more episodes that dealt with "kid stuff." Instead, the stories revolved around us prepping for college, driving, getting jobs, and we even filmed one that had me moving out on my own into a tiny little apartment.

In *Wally's Practical Joke,* Wally and Eddie get back at Lumpy for putting smoke bombs in their cars. The plan was to chain the rear-end of Lumpy's car to a tree and then lure him out of the house by pretending to be a cute girl from school who needed help with her homework. *Heh, heh, heh!*

When Lumpy takes off to meet the girl, the rear-end unexpectedly – and incidentally, unrealistically – breaks off from the back of the car and ends up in the driveway. Eddie and Wally must then right the wrong by reinstalling it on the car.

There were two distinct things I remember about

doing that show. In one of the scenes, Eddie is under the car, trying to check the rear-end oil level. He pulls out the drain plug and ends up with a face full of oil. The special effects folks tried several times to use chocolate syrup to simulate the oil, but they just couldn't get it right. In the end, they refilled the rear-end with *actual* oil, and I had to take a face full of it. That would have never happened today with all of the laws that are in place to protect actors.

But I would have taken a whole bath in oil if it could have prevented what came next. Because the second thing I remember distinctly about filming that episode was when the big news came down from Connelly and Mosher - we were being cancelled.

Eddie Haskell Trivia answer, Chapter 10:
In order to escort his date to the Academy Awards
in style, Ken Osmond had Dayton rent a chauffeur's
uniform and drive them in his brand new 1962
Mercedes Benz 190D. No one – including Ken's
date - realized that the chauffeur was his brother.

Eddie Haskell Trivia Chapter 11: The "rapid-rear-
end removal" gag from Wally's practical joke was
duplicated in what hit movie exactly a decade later?
Answer at end of Chapter 12

TWELVE
"THAT'S A WRAP!"

Even though Norse mythology wasn't a part of the curriculum at North Hollywood High school, I was always interested in the military and in great battles, and I remember reading once about the Valkyrie. A mythical goddess, she was known as the "chooser of the slain" and would fly over the battlefield to decide who would die, and who would live.

I think that there's not just one, but actually two Valkyries. One of them, the traditional one, flies over the true battlefield of bullets and broadswords. And the second one, the one that affects me, flies over the chaotic and bloodied battlefield that is Hollywood. This Valkyrie decides which child actors will go on to act again, and which ones will not. In 1963, I think that Valkyrie flew right past me.

Leave It to Beaver ended when Jerry Mathers realized he had enough of acting, and wanted to go to high school and lead a regular life for a change. Even though part of me was feeling like the show could have gone on, in reality, it had run its course. I have to give credit to Connelly and Mosher also for not wanting to try to milk the show to ridiculous extremes by replacing Jerry, or even worse, pulling the same goofy stunt similar to the show *My Three Sons* did several years later. As each original son left the show for one reason or another, a new one was magically grafted into it to keep true to the title.

We wrapped with a cast and crew party that was very nice for the time, but nothing compared to the extravaganzas that TV shows put on today. Afterward we all said good-bye and went our separate ways. Jerry headed off to get ready for high school. Frank, while still keeping his toe dipped in the acting pond, continued studying at UCLA toward his degree in economics. And Barbara, Hugh, Tony, and I all hit the streets to try to scare up some work.

I was a twenty-year-old, out of work actor, with only a high school degree, and now it was back to the grind for me. I hadn't been on an audition in nearly five years, and it was scary. It was the summer of 1963, pilot season had already been completed, and the shows had been mostly cast. Still, I hoped that I might be able to get a bit part that could evolve into a series regular, or at least recurring role that could keep me busy for a few more years. I soon found out that it wasn't going to be an easy row to hoe.

Typecasting doesn't really hit you all at once; it works on you slowly and subtly, eroding your spirit as you sit by the phone, waiting for the callback that never comes. I went on lots of auditions, and I had lots of rejections. Sometimes I would walk into the room and the casting agent would blurt out, "Hey, you're Eddie Haskell aren't you? Well, I'm afraid it won't work out, nobody can forget you."

The irony to this statement was, I had already been forgotten by one lagging indicator of celebrity; the fan mail I used to receive while the show was in prime time had already started to dry up. They can never forget you? Yeah right, they already were.

Other times, the casting agents wouldn't verbalize it, but I just knew what they were thinking. You see, unlike with the warriors' Valkyrie, the Hollywood version didn't let you know that you were going to die immediately; you were baited, strung along, and then let down to die a slow, lingering death. And like every actor, you would keep telling yourself that success was just around the next bend, but it would be just more empty tracks.

I wasn't the only *Beaver* casualty; Hugh Beaumont who had been very successful before coming to the show by playing tough guys, found that the Ward Cleaver role had softened his image too much to have him taken seriously as a heavy. He would eventually leave acting for good, and open a Christmas tree farm in Minnesota.

Barbara made an attempt at finding more work, but finally saw the writing on the wall as well. She decided to go off to travel Europe instead. However, years later she did her classic portrayal of a jive-talking matron in the comedy movie *Airplane*.

Frank Bank did a pilot for a show based upon the Archie comic-book series, but found that he was directed to act too much like Lumpy on the show, and not as Archie would have. Disgusted, he quit acting and decided to devote all of his energy to bond and stock trading, which ultimately became his long suit.

Of all of us, Tony did the best and got bit parts on several shows including *Dr. Kildare*, *Mr. Novak*, and *Adam 12*. A couple of years later, he and Jerry actually had a fairly successful dinner theatre show titled *So Long Stanley*. Still, it wouldn't be too many years before the same reality we all had experienced hit him in the face and he turned to construction to make a living.

As far as my fortunes, I did score one bit part on the TV show *Petticoat Junction*, but it was the only thing I was able to get.

Thanks to being raised by depression-era parents, I had always been good with saving money and was able to squeak through the year. I had a meager income from the army reserves, so that helped too. *Leave It to Beaver* had already gone into syndication, and I would soon be getting residuals for the episodes I appeared in – but only for six airings, then the *Beaver* well would run dry. Things were getting lean, and I had to wonder; was Eddie Haskell to Ken Osmond what he had been to Wally Cleaver - at times his best friend, but mostly, his biggest nemesis? *Heh, heh, heh!*

* * *

With no regular roles or big parts to sustain me, I took a job at Rocketdyne in nearby Canoga Park. Rocketdyne was an aerospace company that had been spun off from North American Aviation. They designed rocket engines for the burgeoning space program and for military ICBMs. My girlfriend at the time, Jeannie, worked there as a keypunch operator, and she helped me get the job. My job title was blue-printer, but it didn't mean that I was designing cutting-edge rocket engines on blueprints. I was basically a copier, and would convert pencil drawings from the draftsmen into blueprints. It was mindless, uninspiring work, but it was a job and a steady paycheck.

Between my reserve duty, and what few acting parts I could wrangle, I worked there pretty much full time for a year, mostly on the night shift. One morning I came dragging home to find Dayton waiting up for me.

"You ready to quit that dead-end job of yours and come work with me?" he said.

"Doing what?" I asked.
"Flying helicopters."
"Hell yes," I said.

Eddie Haskell Trivia answer, Chapter 11: The 1973 movie, American Graffiti used the same "rip the rear-end out of the car" gag that was used in the "Wally's Practical Joke" episode.

Eddie Haskell Trivia Chapter 12: Ken Osmond will always remember the day he first went to apply for unemployment after Leave It to Beaver ended. It was a very significant day for America and for the world. What was the significant event? Hint: It was in November 1963.
Answer at end of Chapter 13

THIRTEEN
HELICOPTERS UNLIMITED INC.

My brother Dayton had always been what you could term a "wheeler-dealer." After he had gotten his pilot's license, he was still unable to afford the helicopter rental time he needed to be get his commercial rating. Undeterred, he worked out a cozy little arraignment with a flight instructor that allowed him to trade work in exchange for flight time to build up the required hours. In short order, he was soloing and teaching me how to fly. I would never be able to legally take passengers up on my own, but I could share in the pilot duties if it was just the two of us.

By the spring of 1964, we were two flyboys ready to hang out our shingle, and start our charter service. But all we had going for our shoestring operation was Dayton's license and commercial rating, and we didn't have enough money to buy an aircraft. So we did what most fledgling outfits did at the time; we leased one.

It was called a Hiller UH-12B model. It was a two seat, (although we could squeeze three in) piston-powered aircraft that was based upon a trainer built for the US Navy. Some of its forerunners had seen service in the Korean War performing evacuations and observation. Hopefully, we wouldn't be doing any battlefield evacuations, but we would be doing anything and everything else we could to make a buck.

Before long, the work began to come our way. We towed banners, did aerial surveying, photography, night lighting, and sometimes we would fly the local homecoming queen into the stock car races or football game. Through our entertainment industry and motorcycle connections, we would do medical transport for *The Viewfinders*, which was a studio-based motorcycle cross-country club.

Our Hiller UH-12B

We also did work that was a lot less exotic, but very profitable. North of Los Angeles in the city of Thousand Oaks, there was an animal theme park called *Jungleland.* Originally created in 1926 by Luis Goebel, it was an animal support facility for the movie studios. It initially started out with only five lions, but soon the one hundred seventy acre facility was housing all kinds of famous Hollywood animals: Leo, the MGM lion, Mr. Ed the talking horse, even Bimbo, the elephant from the *Circus Boy* TV show I had worked on.

At some point in the facility's history, someone got the bright idea that animals were a big draw, and that with just a little bit of showcasing and some entertainment, families would flock to the park to spend the day, and their money.

Dayton and I would fly the Heller out there on the weekends and do what was called "ride-hopping." For $10 apiece, we would fly up to two passengers on a short aerial tour of the park. We made good money, but they were long days with no guarantee that we would have any passengers. We didn't think it wasn't going to make us rich. For that, we turned to an old standby with deep pockets, the television and movie industry.

As television and movies grew in popularity and sophistication, producers began to rely more and more on aerial shots to create dramatic effect. This was especially true for commercial work, which had only a few seconds to catch the viewer's attention. And nothing did that better than a bird's eye view. Through his work as a prop man and set-builder at the studios, Dayton saw firsthand the business opportunity that someone with a helicopter could capitalize on. We started knocking on doors and calling in every favor we could in the industry.

But studio work demanded a better airship, so we upgraded to a Bell-47. This was the civilian version of the H-13 that you see in the movie and the TV show, *MASH*. It was also used on the classic TV show *Whirlybirds*, which coincidentally Dayton had worked on at one point in his acting career. See what I mean when I say that the Osmond family could never totally escape the TV and film industry?

We did work on the popular TV show *The Fugitive* and commercial shots for Chevrolet and Coca-Cola. We even transported our ship out to the desert near the US/Mexican border once to do work on a Hollywood film. I remember it was the summer and extremely hot. So hot in fact that the air was too thin, and the helicopter blades couldn't grab enough air to get us off the ground. That wasn't our finest moment, or our most memorable. That came on February 2, 1965.

* * *

We were doing video aerial work for a TV show up in Malibu Canyon. Ironically, this is the location where the same shots were taken of the Bell-47 when MASH episodes were filming up there. Producers can be demanding, and that day they had us doing all kinds of things with the helicopter that you should not do. But they were the bosses, and if you wanted to work in this town, you did what they said, and kept your mouth shut and your fingers crossed.

Dayton was flying that day, and I was outboard, meaning I was sitting on the outside of the aircraft and filming. You had to sit on the outside of the craft to avoid getting glare from the canopy on the camera shots. A small seat was mounted on one of the skids and I was sitting in it with a Tyler camera mount in front of me. The mount was essentially a pole to which you mounted the camera.

At the end of the day we had wrapped all of the shots,

and we landed to have the ship serviced and the fuel topped off before we headed home to Whiteman Airport in Pacoima, thirty miles away.

In order to mount the outboard seat on the aircraft, the right hand inside seat would have to be removed. This meant that I would have to stay in the outboard seat for the ride home. It didn't really bother me though; it was unseasonably hot that day, and the breeze felt good sitting out there.

At over 90 MPH, we quickly crossed over the Santa Monica Mountains and were lining up for the approach at Whiteman. In the near distance I could see the tarmac, and the shimmering waves of heat rising up from it. In just a few minutes, we would have landed, had the ship secured, and I would be heading on home. I could already taste the cold beer waiting for me.

Then the engine quit.

Eddie Haskell Trivia answer Chapter 12: Ken Osmond was driving down to the unemployment office and heard on his car radio that President John F. Kennedy had been assassinated.

Eddie Haskell Trivia Chapter 13: Besides being featured in the shows MASH and Whirlybirds, the Bell-47 got its start in television where?
Answer at end of Chapter 14

FOURTEEN
THE INTERSECTION OF HADDON & MONTAGUE, PACOIMA, CALIFORNIA

Unlike a fixed wing aircraft, a helicopter has no glide ratio – zero, zip, nada. So when the engine quits, you fall like a rock. The only saving grace is what's known as the "auto-rotate" feature. Essentially, you disengage the main rotor from the engine and allow it to free-spin, similar to putting a car into neutral. The effect is that the rotor spin will slow you down and allow you to *hopefully* walk away unscathed - but you better do it quickly!

I thank God that Dayton was Johnny-on-the-Spot that day because we were only 200 feet above the ground when the engine quit. If we didn't auto-rotate fast, in just over three seconds we would be smacking into the ground at over 60 MPH. No beer for me.

Dayton Osmond,
"The Tyler camera mount was essentially just like a
spear and it was right in front of Ken. I was so
worried that if we hit too hard it would go right into

his chest and kill him."

The auto-rotation of the main blades slowed us down to a less lethal speed, but that was only half the battle. We still had to find a place to land – and it wasn't going to be easy, we were over the busy intersection of Haddon and Montague. Dayton picked a spot in the middle to put it down, but just then, a car went through.

Dayton Osmond,
"I had to try to avoid the car and when I did, we
heard a big crashing sound."

The main rotors of the helicopter caught part of a power line and this threw us down hard, nose first. We missed hitting any cars, but still, it wasn't a good landing. I got out of my seat and stood up, I was covered in blood…or at least I thought it was blood.

The crash had severed the hydraulic lines of the helicopter, and the red fluid had sprayed all over me. I checked myself for injury but I found none. By now, horns were honking all over the place and people were getting out of their cars to see if we were okay. Someone ran to a nearby pay phone to call the police. It was pandemonium.

Dayton unhooked his seatbelt and ran around to check on me. I knew he would think the same thing as me when he saw me covered in red, so I said, "I'm okay, it's just the fluid."

Like any pilot, your first responsibility is to the safety of your crew, then to the general public. Dayton and I did a quick check for fires or fuel leaks on the ship; we found none. In the distance we could hear sirens racing to the scene. Then Dayton went into shock and he collapsed in front of me.

The newspaper article about our crash.

"Pilot error" is the death knell of any pilot's career. The cause of our crash was determined as failure of engine due to lack of fuel. We knew that we had topped off the tank in Malibu, and we should have had a good two and a half hours of safe flying time. Instead, we ran out after only thirty-five minutes. But since we had used our own service truck to top us off, instead of buying fuel at the airport, which would have provided us with a receipt, we had no proof of how much fuel we had put into the tank. It was our word against the Federal Aviation Administration. Because of this, Dayton's license was suspended, and we weren't able to fly. Unless something exonerated us, our business was kaput.

Our redemption came from the very same airship several months later. After the crash, the Bell-47 was not considered a total loss. It was soon rebuilt, deemed airworthy, and went right back into service. A flight instructor fueled up the ship one day at Whiteman Airport and took off for a training flight. She made it no further than the end of the runway before the engine ran out of fuel on her. With a receipt to prove it, the ship was taken out of service and the culprit was found in the form of a failure in the carburetor on the engine. Apparently, with all of our shenanigans that day flying in Malibu Canyon, we had dislodged something that was causing the ship to gulp down fuel like no one's business. Dayton's license was reinstated.

We got another helicopter and tried to make up for lost time, but unlike our physical beings, our business was mortally wounded from the crash, and we were never able to recover. We lasted about another year and then said adios to the helicopter charter business. My stint as a fly-boy was over. Again, I was back to the grind looking for work.

Eddie Haskell Trivia answer, Chapter 13:
Besides being featured in the shows MASH and
Whirlybirds, the Bell-47 got its start in television in
Episode 140 of the iconic show I Love Lucy when
Lucille Ball had to be lowered onto a cruise ship
from the ubiquitous helicopter. Desilu Studios was
so impressed with the performance of the craft, they
decided to create a show around it. And so,
Whirlybirds was born.

Eddie Haskell Trivia Chapter 14: While trying to
rebuild their helicopter business, Ken and his
brother attempted to pull together enough financing
to get a Bell Jet Ranger helicopter, which was one
of the hottest airships of the time. A famous TV
actor was interested in becoming a silent partner in
the venture. Who was the actor?
Answer at end of Chapter 15

FIFTEEN
SANDY PURDY...
AND A LOVE OF MOTORCYCLES

I've always had a love of motorcycles. Even when
the 1937 Cushman that Dayton and I pushed home when
we were kids caught on fire, I still loved it. Even when
he lane split with me on the back, and I would get flung
off because my knees hit the cars on either side, I loved
it. And when the first Honda motorcycles came off the
boat in Los Angeles in the early sixties, Dayton and I
were the first ones in line to buy one.

I was a member of a motorcycle club. Mind you, we
weren't Hell's Angel gangs or anything like that, we
were just a group of people who loved to get together
and ride. My girlfriend Jeannie was a member of the
same club as me. One morning, we rode over to the
International House Of Pancakes restaurant in Van Nuys
on my new Harley, to meet up with some fellow
members, that's where I met her.

Her maiden name was Sandy Purdy, and she had
attended North Hollywood High School. Even though
we went at the same time, she was several grades behind

me so we never really associated. Her brother Vance was in my class and I knew him, but otherwise, we had no connection other than being in the same motorcycle club together. Her boyfriend at the time was Bruce Smith, and he rode in the club as well. Sandy loved riding with him although she didn't have her own motorcycle. Both of these facts would soon change.

> *Sandy Osmond,*
> *"I remember that Bruce and I had gone on a motorcycle run up to Big Bear Lake, about two hours away from Los Angeles. And I remember that he took off and just left me sitting there, waiting for hours. I realized then that he was a jerk and that I didn't want to keep dating him, so I broke off our relationship."*

Even though Sandy broke up with Bruce, that didn't mean she was going to give up riding. She had been a horse person all of her life, and felt that the two hobbies were kindred in many ways. Not wanting to have to depend on anyone else, she saved her money and bought a Triumph 650 from a man in Burbank – with the stipulation that he would teach her how to ride it.

Sandy's Triumph and my Harley were both featured in Modern Cycle Magazine.

Not only did Sandy start riding on her own with the group; she began showing her motorcycle as well. Her father, and her brother Vance, were both very handy, and after her parents got over the initial shock of their daughter getting a motorcycle, they helped her disassemble the Triumph, repaint it in a gold spider web design, and chrome several of the components.

She started competing and was doing very well. In

the meantime, I would see her at the meets and shows, and I really began to become attracted to her. Finally one day, I got up the nerve to ask her out.

> *Sandy Osmond,*
> *"I remember Ken asked me out for coffee one evening. We took his car, had some coffee, and then he took me to this nice lookout point that looked down over the San Fernando Valley. He then proceeded to see how far he could get with me until I stopped him and asked, 'What about Jeannie?' To which he replied, 'Jeannie who?'"*

I confessed at that point that I had broken up with Jeannie and that I wanted to start dating her. And so we did, although at times our burgeoning relationship had some interesting moments.

Even though I was flying with Dayton, hoping against hope, I still kept my feelers out for acting jobs, and occasionally I'd get one. I did a *Munster's* episode in 1966, and another *Lassie* episode. Then I got a bit part in a lousy B movie *C'mon, Let's Live a Little* in 1967. My character's name was "The Beard," and boy, was it apropos. They had me in a long hair wig and a big old beard. I looked like something out of a ZZ Top music video.

Sandy and I had made a date to have lunch, and I was supposed to meet her Aunt Gloria and Uncle Bill for the first time. But the studio had me in full makeup and I couldn't take it off, so I ended up having to go over looking like that. I'm sure they must have been shocked and thought, "What the heck is Sandy thinking, dating this bum?"

That was a very comical memory from our relationship, some were far more acrimonious.

Sandy Osmond,
"It was very iffy for quite a while because Ken
would kind of bounce back and forth between
Jeannie and I. It was very uncomfortable too as I
would have to see Jeannie at the club meets and
rides."

Sandy and I would have never made it, had it not been for two other people that were in the motorcycle club with us. Their names were Bud and Dottie Priest. They were the elders of the club, and very much like parents to a lot of us. They knew what was going on, and knew that Sandy and I were meant for each other, in spite of my shenanigans to the contrary.

Sandy and I on my custom blue Harley 74 .

In the end, I realized that Sandy was the one for me. We got back together and to celebrate the renewal of our relationship I said, "Hey, why don't we take a cross country trip on my Harley?"
And so that's what we did.

Eddie Haskell Trivia answer, Chapter 14: Dan Blocker, the gentle giant who played Hoss Cartwright on the iconic TV western, Bonanza was going to become a silent partner in the Osmond's helicopter business. Unfortunately, the deal fell through.

Eddie Haskell Trivia Chapter 15: What did Sandy Purdy do to immortalize the cross-country motorcycle trip she took with Ken?
Answer at end of Chapter 16

SIXTEEN
RETURN TO GOTEBO

In the early morning of July 2, 1966, Sandy and I began what would be, for both of us, the longest ride we had ever done on a motorcycle. My custom blue Harley 74 was loaded to the gills with saddlebags, a "scootboot," and a suitcase mounted on top of the scootboot. We were packed for three weeks of cross-country travel, and with both us on the bike; we weighed in at a whopping 1,200 pounds!

A friend took off with us that morning and escorted us as far as California's Mojave Desert. After that, we were on our own. By late afternoon, we hit our first major point of interest, the Grand Canyon. Even against the backdrop of such remarkable scenery, the Harley became quite an attraction, and we were held up with people wanting to talk about the bike and take pictures.

By the end of the first day, we had covered seven hundred miles and landed in Winslow, Arizona where we *did not* stand on a corner – we were just too tired.

Our relationship was very solid by this time, and we got along great on the trip. We traveled through New

Mexico and Texas, and then reached Oklahoma by the third day. We stopped in Gotebo and Sandy met some of my surviving relatives, including my maternal grandmother.

The first day of our road trip, at the California/Arizona border.

After a side trip to the Ozarks, our jaunt continued on into Kansas and Missouri, where Sandy not only met more of my extended family, but also was amazed by a sight she had never before seen, or was expecting.

Sandy Osmond,
"Fireflies! I just couldn't believe it. I was a
California girl born and raised, and we just didn't
have them out there. They were just incredible!"
It was also during this time that a subject came up

that I should have been expecting, but nevertheless, it still took me by surprise: marriage.

* * *

Three weeks and five thousand miles later, we returned to California. Sandy went back to her job working as a secretary at Lockheed, and I tried to scare up any work I could. The residuals from *Beaver* had just about dried up and, hopelessly typecast, I was unable to secure anything other than bit parts in TV shows and films. I needed a steady job.

> *Sandy Osmond,*
> *"I honestly didn't know what Ken did for a living. I knew about his acting on the show, and when I first met him he was flying helicopters. But after the crash, I knew that that was over. He always seemed to have money though. I guess I was so in love with him I was pretty naïve. (laughing) He could have been a bank robber for all I knew."*

My final acting gig of the sixties came in the 1968 movie, *With Six You Get Eggroll*, a comedy starring Doris Day and Brian Keith. I had a bit part and made a couple of bucks. That was all. If I were ever going to get anywhere in life, acting would have to take a backseat to a real job. Ironically, I found myself never straying too far away from the industry that my family had been tied to all of those years. I stopped looking for acting jobs and became a prop maker for the studios.

* * *

Like my father had before me, I joined the Theatrical Stage Employees Union Local 44 and began working at the various studios. I worked on shows such as *The Flying Nun* staring Sally Field, but for the most part you never really knew much about what show you were working on. You were told to build a wall here or there and you did, hastily – after all, it only had to look good for fifteen minutes.

While not being terribly lucrative, I was still able to save a decent amount of money during that time. I was still living at home and realized that when I moved out I didn't want to be beholden to a landlord by renting. I wanted to purchase a home for Sandy and me, so I began looking.

After a short time, I found just the money-pit I was looking for. The house was on Vineland Avenue in nearby Sun Valley. The home was built in 1952 and had been a rental for a long time. It had sat empty for over year by the time I found it, and had been broken into and vandalized. It was a wreck, required $2,500 down to purchase, and was just what I was looking for.

> *Sandy Osmond,*
> *"My heart sank when I first saw it. It was absolutely horrible. Still, Ken assured me that we could fix it up and so I worked with him to come up with the down payment. He had saved $2000 and so I sold some of my horse gear and tack to come up with the rest."*

Building a wall, or putting in a door or window for a movie set was one thing, rehabbing a house so that it wouldn't fall down in the first stiff breeze was quite another. To this end, Sandy's father, Grandpa Purdy helped immensely. He had been an aerospace engineer and was incredibly talented when it came to all things mechanical.

And so, every moment that I had available was spent

working on the house, either with Grandpa or by myself. To Sandy and everyone else looking from the outside in, it seemed that this was the natural progression, and that I was building our little love-nest for us to get married and live happily ever after in. The only one who wasn't onboard with the idea was me.

I was admittedly, terrified of marriage. I don't know why, because I loved Sandy to death, and I knew that I wanted to spend the rest of my life with her. I was just a "commitment-phobe" I guess. She would want to talk about it and make plans, and I would try to shift the subject away. It worked for the most part, but one evening I found myself in a situation even I couldn't wriggle out of.

Eddie Haskell Trivia answer, Chapter 15: In order to immortalize the cross-country motorcycle trip that she took with Ken, Sandy wrote an article for Harley Enthusiast Magazine and had it published.

Eddie Haskell Trivia Chapter 16: Besides Ken acting in the movie, With Six You Get Eggroll, what did he and Sandy both contribute to the film? Answer at the end of Chapter 17

SEVENTEEN
THE QUESTION

Sandy Osmond,
"Ken spent lots of time at my parent's house and
was very close to both of them. One night, he was
over at our house having dinner with my family and
my mom raised the obvious question, 'So, just when
are the two of you getting married?'

I thought it was reasonable question and so I said,
'Well I think June is a great month. What do you
think Ken?"

Sandy later told me that I had literally gone white. I sat there, speechless, at the Purdy family dinner table. I felt as trapped physically as I was by the question and the topic. Eventually, I guess I mumbled something about that sounding good, but Sandy could tell by my bearing that this was not going to go well.

Sandy Osmond,
That's when I realized he was terrified. He had

been reticent before whenever I brought up the subject, but he was a man of few words anyway. Now I knew that we had a big problem on our hands."

I don't know what was wrong with me, because I loved her, knew that I didn't want anyone else, and that I would be happy to spend the rest of my life with her. But the "M" word just changed everything in me. After we got away from her family, we had a long talk. In fact, we had several long talks over the next couple of months that never seemed to get me any closer to committing. Finally, Sandy had had enough and told me in no uncertain terms.

Sandy Osmond,
"I hope you and your house are happy Ken. Good-bye."

I was devastated. Just like Eddie Haskell, I was mucking up a great thing. But this wasn't acting, this wasn't a script, and there were no re-takes. It was real. I was going to lose the woman of my dreams forever unless I did something drastic…and it better be soon.

Sandy Osmond,
"Ken began writing me love letters, dozens of them. He would mail them to my house and even leave them on my car at work. They were wonderful, heartfelt letters. I never realized he had such emotion in him. But they were just words – not deeds, and I wouldn't budge. I wouldn't speak to him on the phone or come to the door if he came over."

Even with pouring out my heart and soul to Sandy, it

seemed hopeless; she was slipping even further away from me. I needed some intervention from a third party. I called on Dottie Priest, who had saved our relationship the first time.

Sandy Osmond,
"I had a great deal of respect for Dottie, but even with her counseling, I resisted getting back with Ken. I wanted to have a real marriage and a real family with kids and all that; I wasn't just going to live together. If Ken couldn't handle that, then he would have to find someone else."

Sandy and I in her parent's house.

But I didn't want anyone else; I wanted, loved, and needed Sandy. It took a lot of shuttle diplomacy on Dottie's part, but she finally got us together. I was ready to commit to her for the rest of my life. We set a date.

Eddie Haskell Trivia answer, Chapter 16: Sandy and Ken both had their motorcycles, her Triumph and his Harley, featured in the movie "With Six, You Get Eggroll." While on the set, Sandy struck up a conversation with Doris Day, without even realizing who she was.

Eddie Haskell Trivia Chapter 17: Of the main characters on the Leave It to Beaver show, how many have never been divorced?
Answer at the end of Chapter 18

EIGHTEEN
JUNE 28, 1969

It was like a switch flipped in me.

Sandy and I were married on June 28, 1969. The church was in nearby Glendale, California, the same city I had been born in twenty-six years prior. With neither of us having rich parents to lavish an elaborate wedding ceremony on us, we had to keep it very simple – and so we did.

Our reception was held in the basement of the church and consisted of only punch and wedding cake. The cake itself had been baked and decorated by none other than Dottie Priest, the woman who worked so tirelessly to bring us, and then keep us, together. Sandy had a very simple wedding band with an inscription, "KO & SO" inside of it. And her wedding dress was an "off the rack" affair. My brother Dayton served as co-best man, along with Sandy's brother Vance, whom I was very close to.

One thing that was very important to me was that my mom, who was still being cared for at the Motion Picture & Television Country House and Hospital, was able to be at my wedding.

Our wedding day.

After the ceremony and reception, we went to Sandy's parent's house for a brief time and then took off on our honeymoon, which was also spartan, but we did it with panache.

Sandy Osmond,
"We had a wonderful time, both at our wedding and on our honeymoon. My parents had a friend who owned a nice cabin up at Big Bear Lake, about two

hours east of Los Angeles. They let us stay there for free. Our friends decorated our car with "JUST MARRIED" signs, and we drove up to the mountains in style."

At the reception with our parents: Ed and Mary Purdy, Thurman and Pearl Osmond.

We returned home a couple of days later to our fixer-upper house on Vineland Avenue, crazy in love with one another, and ready to set up house. I had to ask myself, what I had been so afraid of; Sandy was the only woman for me, and I wanted to spend the rest of my life with her. Still, love only takes you so far and doesn't pay the bills. We were very poor, and struggled through the first year.

Our good friend C.A. had an old sofa he gave to us. Other people gave us cast-offs as well. We used milk crates and concrete blocks with pieces of particleboard for shelves. We didn't even have a kitchen table and had to use TV trays. We were like most couples just starting out, rich with our love, but poor otherwise. We ate the cheapest food we could find, and scrimped and saved everywhere we could. Still, we had faith that we were heading in the right direction, and even continued to improve upon the house where we could. Sometimes though, the house plans didn't exactly go as expected.

Sandy Osmond,
"Our first Christmas after being married, I asked Ken what he wanted. Since the front door to our home was essentially shot, he said, 'How about if we just get a new front door for the house?' I thought it was a great idea, so he gave me the dimensions: 36 inches. Except door measurements aren't written like that, so when I took the measurements to a door supplier, they interpreted them as 3-6, or three feet, six inches!

The man at the store repeatedly asked me if these were correct, because it was a very odd size and it would be special order, and I said 'Yes, my husband took the measurements himself.' So I ordered it, a custom made 42 inch door!"

I remember that Sandy had it all wrapped up with a bow and ribbon, and when she showed it to me, she could tell by my expression that something was wrong.

"Don't you like it?" she asked.

"I love it," I said. "There's just one problem, it's too big."

After we figured out what had happened, she felt terrible. We had an expensive, custom-made door that we couldn't return. I grabbed a tape measure and measured the front opening of the house.

"Don't worry," I said. "I'll make it fit."

And so on the morning of December 26, 1969, hammer in hand, I began enlarging the front opening of our house for our custom-made 42-inch door, bow and all.

* * *

Even though I was able to make an oversized door fit our home, I still wasn't able to make our undersized wages fit our budget. By January of 1970, a change would be coming that would dramatically affect our lives forever, financially and otherwise. The change had its genesis in the oddest of circumstances. The change occurred because of *Fraulein Mugwomp.*

> *Eddie Haskell Trivia answer Chapter 17 Only one member of the Leave It to Beaver cast has never been divorced: Ken Osmond.*

> *Eddie Haskell Trivia: Besides the oversized door incident, Sandy and Ken experienced another very comical blunder with regards to improving their home. What was it?*
> *Answer at end of Chapter 19*

NINETEEN
FRAU MUGWOMP, AND LA'S FINEST

Fraulein Mugwomp was the pet name of Sandy's 1956 Mercedes Benz SL convertible. Back then, it was just an old used car to us, but today it would be a collector's item. It was extremely unreliable, and even though I did most of the repairs, it was still costing us far too much money. We needed to get something more reliable. She had paid $500 for it, and based upon what information we could find about what they were going for, we thought we could make a few bucks.

We listed it for $650, and after a few days of running the ad, an attorney who had just passed the bar came by to look at it. While he was there, somehow the subject came up about jobs and the police department. I told him that I would love to work for the Los Angeles Police Department, but that I didn't make the weight requirement, which at the time, was a whopping 140 pounds. I only weighed 135 pounds, soaking wet.

The attorney told me that I should follow my dreams, and that if it was only a matter of five pounds, I could really do it if I put my mind to it.

He purchased the car and a couple of days later I

applied for LAPD. Then I embarked on one of the most bizarre campaigns of my life, I set out to gorge myself to gain the five pounds I needed to become an LAPD officer.

> *Tony Dow,*
> *"I remember seeing Kenny during that time, and he was eating everything and drinking milk shakes all the time. He was so sick of eating."*

I ate constantly, almost every hour on the hour; nine meals a day with snacks in between. And I weighed myself every day, hoping to see a huge change. It was happening, but slowly, maybe a pound every other week or so.

In the meantime, I went in and took my written exam, which I passed with flying colors. Then it was the oral and the psyche; they went fine as well. It was all coming down to the physical, which was coming up fast.

April 19, 1970 was a Thursday. I took a vacation day from my job as a prop maker and went down to take my physical. Our bathroom scale at home read 140 pounds...maybe it said 141. I couldn't be sure, and I couldn't take a chance.

Just before I left to go in to LAPD headquarters, I grabbed a brand new half-gallon milk container out of our refrigerator.

"What's that for?" Sandy asked me as I was heading out the door.

"Insurance," I said.

I hadn't gone to the bathroom since I got up that morning and on the way down to the station chugged down the whole half gallon of milk. My bladder was already hurting and I hoped I could get through it without an accident.

By the time I finally got called into the examination

room, my bladder was on the verge of thermo-nuclear explosion. Slowly and methodically, the doctor went through my blood pressure, respiration, eyes, ears, nose, throat…everything except my weight. Why couldn't he do that first? I was about to detonate!

Finally, he said the words I had been waiting hours to hear.

"Okay, step on the scale please."

Wearing just my underwear I stepped onto it. He slid the large counter-weight to the 100-pound position, and then slowly began tapping the smaller one over. I was about to burst, both from anticipation and hydraulic pressure.

…38…39…40…41…42

The indicator needle on the far end of the scale hovered in between its stops. The doctor stopped moving the weight and looked up at me.

"One hundred forty-two," he said. "You passed."

Then he smiled a knowing grin at me and said, "You can go pee now."

I bet I was in the bathroom for a half an hour.

Eddie Haskell Trivia answer Chapter 18. Besides the oversized door debacle at Sandy and Ken's home, the young couple also bought a bedroom set that had a dresser that they couldn't open because of doors that hit the side of their bed. Ken and his hammer came to the rescue again by building a whole new bedroom. They still have the bedroom set to this day.

Eddie Haskell Trivia Chapter 19: Ken and Sandy sold their 1956 Mercedes Benz SL convertible for $650. If they had held onto it, what would it be worth today?
Answer at end of Chapter 20

TWENTY
LAPD ACADEMY, ELYSIAN PARK, LOS ANGELES

I didn't care how much my bladder had to suffer that day; I had made it and was accepted to go to the LAPD Academy. My final day as a prop maker was on Friday, May 15. I started the academy the following Monday on May 18. It was like I was stepping into another world.

The academy sits on approximately twenty-one acres in Elysian Park, just north of downtown Los Angeles. Just a stone's throw away is Chavez Ravine, home of Dodger Stadium. The academy was created in 1935 as a means to provide formal training to LAPD officers. Before it was built, new recruits who passed the minimum requirements for the department were simply given a gun and a badge, and told to keep the city safe. You either learned real quickly on the job, or you died trying.

The academy grounds themselves are picturesque and bucolic, and contain numerous fountains, flower gardens, and waterfalls. The classrooms and training buildings are, in keeping with the history of Los Angeles, Spanish-style architecture with arches and tile roofs. It was beautiful, but I didn't have much time to enjoy it. This was like army basic training all over again...only worse.

Just like the military, the purpose of basic training is not only to train you, but also to push you to see if you'll break. The herd is thinned in this manner to hopefully keep both the police, and the public, safe from those who are not up to the task.

We ran seven miles every day and did calisthenics on top of that. I was very good at doing push-ups, pull-ups, and sit-ups, but the running really took it out of me. There was a very tall staircase near the academy grounds that was in a scene from the classic Laurel and Hardy film, *The Music Box*. We had to run up those stairs every single day. They just about killed me. And then there was "punishment hill."

Punishment hill was a ridiculously steep hill on the academy grounds. It was given its name because this was what a recruit had to run if they screwed up – and everybody screwed up; the drill instructors made sure of it.

Unlike the military though, at the police academy, academics played a far greater role and are an equal, if not greater, part of the stress that is on you at all times. We had several classes a day, mixed in with our physical training. We learned about the law, about tactics, procedures...every aspect of policing you could think of.

Thankfully, I had a great support system at home. Sandy was with me every step of the way. Every wife essentially goes through the academy training right along with her husband.

> *Sandy Osmond,*
> *"One of the things I remember most about that time was the uniforms. They had to be cleaned and pressed every single day. It seemed as if I was*

constantly washing and ironing."

I pretty much breezed through the academic part of the training and took few if any notes. I paid very good attention. I don't know if it was due to my training as an actor and having to memorize lines or not, but any advantage I could get, I'd take.

And sometimes my experience as an actor not only had advantages, but quite possibly presented unique opportunities for me as well. One day, just a month or so after I started the academy, I was called into one of the offices. Several training officers and some other people I didn't know were in there as well. I had no idea what was going on and thought that maybe I had screwed up.

Then one of them asked me, "Osmond, how'd you like to go undercover for the LAPD?"

* * *

I was stunned, and had no idea how to respond, other than that I had learned in the army that you never refuse an assignment, because it usually helped your career.

"Sure," I said. "What do I have to do?"

"Nothing," another officer said. "At this point anyway. We're going to initiate a more detailed background check, and if it comes back clean, you'll disappear."

"Disappear?" I said.

"You'll be taken out of your academy training class and given special training. You won't graduate like a regular officer. We don't want anybody to ID you. Sound okay?"

"Sure," I said.

"You can return to your class right now while we check things out. Not a word to anyone. Got it?"

"Yes sir."

So I fell back in with my class and kept my mouth shut. I didn't even tell Sandy. A week or so later I was summoned to the same office again. I was hoping to hear the good news. What I heard instead was that unfortunately, my cover was blown.

A reporter for the Valley News had gotten wind of me joining the academy and felt that the incongruity of Eddie Haskell becoming a cop was simply too juicy to ignore, so he wrote a story about it.

So went my brief flirtation with police undercover work. Sometimes Eddie just can't win. It was back to my class and to punishment hill.

* * *

The part of my training that I was most miserable at was the wrestling that they made us do as part of our hand-to-hand combat training. Being smaller than most of the other recruits, I was already at a disadvantage, but to make matters worse my drill instructor took great sadistic pleasure by pairing me with another recruit named Guzman. Guzman was a champion collegiate wrestler. The DI would pair me up with him on the mat and shout, "Go." In two seconds, I would be face first on the mat and unable to breathe.

Graduation day, LAPD

If the DI was attempting to break me on the wrestling mat, my own body was sending its own signals to my brain telling me to quit. About halfway through our training, I developed bone spurs in both of my feet. It was excruciating, but I knew that if I dropped out now, I would have to start the whole cycle all over again, and that was not something I wanted to do.

So I taped my feet up every day and suffered through it. And just like my swollen bladder that got me in there, it was all worth it. On October 9, 1970 twenty weeks after I first stepped foot in Elysian Park, I graduated from the police academy. I was now an Officer for the Los Angeles Police Department. It was *one* of the most momentous days of my life.

A bigger day came just four months later, when I was working the streets and got home from patrol; Sandy was pregnant.

Eddie Haskell Trivia answer Chapter 19: If Ken and Sandy had held onto their 1956 Mercedes Benz SL convertible, Frau Mugwomp, in good condition today, would be worth $90,000.

Eddie Haskell Trivia Chapter 20: While speaking at a writing conference, co-author Christopher J. Lynch happened to meet Ken Osmond's police academy drill instructor, who still remembered the young recruit. What did the instructor have to say about Ken's time in the academy?
Answer at end of Chapter 21

TWENTY-ONE
THE BOYS IN BLUE, AND BABY BLUE

I'm not sure if most cops remember the first call they went on after graduating from the academy, but I remember mine. I had been assigned to a "T" car, or "traffic-car." Our responsibilities were to respond to motor vehicle accidents, make sure no one was injured, that the vehicles were moved out of the road, and that the respective drivers were exchanging information as required by law.

The first call I went with my training officer on, was a garden variety fender-bender. No one was injured and the parties were handling it properly. I remember that one of the drivers came up to me and asked me if his insurance was going to go up because of the accident? I informed him that we had nothing to do with setting insurance rates and that I really couldn't tell him anything about it. He said that he understood, but that with all of my vast experience, maybe I could "guesstimate" what the effect would be on his insurance premiums.

I had ten minutes of "vast" experience as a sworn

peace officer.

Your first year as a new officer is a whirlwind that sweeps you up and blows you around so fast, you never even know what hit you. Every call is a new call, and every day is a new adventure. I loved it and remember the first time I went on vacation; I couldn't wait for my vacation to end so I could get back to work.

I mostly worked patrol that first year, but occasionally got bounced out to traffic. Handling fender-benders was definitely less stressful, but patrol calls were far more interesting, even if they were dangerous. On average, it was necessary for me to draw my service revolver out at least once a shift while doing patrol.

One of our routine calls was to a housing project in Pacoima, a low income and high crime area north of Los Angeles, in the eastern end of the San Fernando Valley. So dangerous was the housing project, there was a standing order that we weren't to respond without a minimum of two, two-person patrol cars...*and* a supervisor!

We responded to all manner of calls there including fights and domestic disturbances. These were often-times very tense calls, but sometimes humorous as well.

On one domestic disturbance call, a man and woman were fighting like cats and dogs. My partner/training officer at the time was very seasoned and had seen it all in his many years on patrol.

"So are you two married?" he asked them, when he could calm them down enough to answer.

"Yes," the man said. "We're common law."

Immediately, my partner and I both knew that they had no idea what they were talking about, because California does not recognize common law marriages. And if they were so ignorant about the legality of their marital status, they were probably just as clueless as to the powers of a peace officer.

"Would you like me to divorce you then?" my partner asked the man.

"Yes!" he said emphatically.

"Okay. Place your hand on my badge."

The man placed his hand on my partner's badge and I watched dumbfounded as I saw,– even with all my years of experience in film and TV, the most convincing bit of acting I had ever seen in my life.

"By the powers vested in me... as a sworn peace officer with the State of California...I now decree your marriage to be null and void..."

And so that's how we handled it. The couple seemed pleased as punch that they were now divorced, and I realized that I was glad my partner never auditioned for the Eddie role – I never would have been picked!

We had other calls that weren't near as violent as the housing project ones, but were still humorous. One of the areas we had to patrol was the Sunland/Tujunga area, known fondly by the officers assigned to it as "The World's Largest Open Air Insane Asylum." It's so crazy there it's even listed in the Urban Dictionary.

Evelyn was a very sweet woman, but she simply couldn't escape the "little people" that were tormenting her by whispering in her head and invading her house. Occasionally, they would drive her to fits and she would smash them with a hammer as they climbed the common wall that she shared with her neighbor. The only problem was, Evelyn's neighbor didn't appreciate the wall being destroyed – little people or not.

My partner received a call at least every other week about Evelyn, who unfortunately was very disturbed and possibly beyond conventional means of reasoning. He therefore, like any good cop, improvised.

After listening to her tell him about the little people who were so disturbing to her, he asked Evelyn if she had any aluminum foil. She did and returned from her kitchen with a roll of it. He turned to me.

"Make Evelyn a hat so that they don't disturb her any longer."

Being a new officer, I did was I was told, and fashioned a hat out of the aluminum foil. When it was done, my partner placed it on her head and pronounced, "There you go Evelyn, as long as you wear that hat, the little people cannot disturb you."

We never got a call about Evelyn again. My partner really knew his stuff!

Party hats and impromptu divorces notwithstanding, your primary job is to protect the public, no matter what the situation. And sometimes the situation comes up when you least expect it, like when you're off duty.

* * *

It was the early morning of February 9, 1971, two months after I graduated the academy. I had just gotten home from work when our house started to shake…and shake…and shake. We were having an earthquake.

In Sylmar, California, only seven miles from where we lived in Sun Valley, a thrust earthquake measuring 6.6 on the Richter Scale occurred, shaking the ground violently for twelve seconds – which is a loooong time if you've ever been in an earthquake!

Surprisingly, our home suffered no damage, other than some things falling off shelves. One of the craziest things I saw though was that our dog, a fully mature Great Dane, actually crawled underneath our couch – which was only three inches high! The couch was balancing on her back.

Immediately, a call went out to all officers to report in to headquarters. All days off were cancelled, and we went to emergency 12-hour shifts indefinitely. I had a bunch of job duties, many of which were very boring since I was low man on the totem pole. I remember having to guard a supermarket that had collapsed to keep it from being looted. The amazing thing was, the supermarket's floor safe had broken loose and had gone right out through the front window of the store and was sitting in the parking lot. There was a perfectly clean trail right behind the safe. It looked like a broom had swept the pathway all the way out.

Other times though, I actually got my hands dirty and helped dig out. There was lots of damage including buildings, freeway overpasses, and the Van Norman Dam where 80,000 people had to be evacuated for four days while the reservoir level could be lowered. Some of the worst damage, and where the majority of the deaths occurred, was at the Veteran's Hospital Facility where four buildings collapsed, killing many of the patients as they slept in their beds. Thankfully, I was never assigned to help with that recovery effort.

After about a month, things settled back to normal, whatever normal is for a new cop. It's tough being on probation, and you always feel like an axe is hanging over your head ready to drop. You know that the department could fire you, without cause, in that first year.

All of this was set against the backdrop of Sandy being pregnant with our first child. Every time I came home from work, it seemed like she was getting bigger and bigger. The big day was looming and I had no idea where I would be, or what I would be doing when it happened. Then the call came in one day from the RTO (radio telephone operator).

"16 Adam 89, phone the station."

I knew what was going on. Whenever private conversations between dispatch and the officers was requested, we used a call-box, otherwise known as a

Gamewell, who was the company that manufactured them. The phone went straight to the station, and bypassed all of the rigmarole you would go through by trying to call on a pay phone – if you could find one that was working.

We found a box close by, and I inserted the long brass key to unlock it, and called in. The watch commander told me that my wife was in labor at St. Joseph's Hospital. I told my partner I had to return to the station.

> *Sandy Osmond,*
> *"I knew that I couldn't wait for Ken to get all the way in from the field and clear headquarters to drive me to the hospital, so I drove myself."*

Time off for an officer is based upon many factors; how much vacation time he has, how much comp time he's accrued, and so forth, but you are ultimately a public servant, and it all comes down to minimum staffing needs to protect the city. It just so happened that we were at the minimum on the day Sandy went into labor, and so the watch commander told me he couldn't give me *any* time off, even though I had plenty on the books.

"Then show me as sick," I said and turned and walked away. I was going to be there when my son was born.

Eric Ed Osmond was born on October 8, 1971. His middle name was in honor of Sandy's father. Back then you didn't know the sex of the baby before it was born, so we had a girl's name picked out as well: Tawny-Dawn.

* * *

After the birth of Eric, Sandy's parents, especially her mom, really helped out. They had been so excited and had been pushing us to produce grandchildren for them, so they finally got their wish.

I got my wish too. After years of up and downs, fill-in jobs and hustling auditions, my life had finally settled out.

I had a steady job, a wife, a child, a house, and a mortgage to make. I was like a million other working stiffs.

Although it had only been about four years since my last gig, acting seemed so long ago. Filming *Leave It to Beaver* episodes was like ancient history to me. I rarely got fan mail any longer, and I was slowly fading into obscurity. No one seemed to remember Eddie Haskell any longer

...or so I thought.

Eddie Haskell Trivia answer Chapter 20: Ken Osmonds's LAPD drill instructor remembers him as being one of the smallest recruits he ever had.

Eddie Haskell Trivia Chapter 21: Why did the LAPD continue to use call-boxes up until the 1990s even though they had a sophisticated, powerful radio transmission system?
Answer at end of Chapter 22

TWENTY-TWO
JOHN HOLMES

"You need to get your butt downtown right now!"

I was in court in Van Nuys, about eighteen miles northwest of downtown Los Angeles, sitting in the little room they keep you in until you're called to testify. I was looking over my notes when he burst into the room. No niceties, no introduction other than flashing me his shield to let me know he was the real deal. I think he was just another officer from headquarters. I had never seen him before, but he let me know who was in charge.

"But I'm under subpoena," I said. "I can't leave until I testify."

"Okay," he said, making no effort to hide his irritation.

"When you're done here, regardless of the time, report to internal affairs."

He stormed out of the waiting room just like he had come in, and I was left speechless. I wondered what I had done wrong, what citizen had made a complaint against me, or what report I had screwed up on. To a cop, the Internal Affairs Department is the devil

146

incarnate, the equivalent of the IRS; nobody ever wants to go see them. At a bare minimum, they could make your life and your career hell, or they could end it completely with nothing more than the stroke of a pen.

I finished with court a couple hours later and headed to Parker Center and internal affairs, having no idea what the hell was going on.

When I got there, I gave the receptionist my name, and she instructed me to sit down and wait.

And that's what I did, for the entire rest of the day.

"Come back here tomorrow," she said. "At nine o'clock."

And so I showed up the next day, and it was the same drill. I sat in the same chair all day long and was told to return once again, the following day. I knew what they were doing; they were stringing me along, making me sweat, so when they finally let me in, I would collapse in a heap of blubbering jelly, begging for forgiveness and confessing all my worldly sins. The only problem with this was, I didn't know what my sins were.

On the third day I waited and waited, until finally they called me in. In many ways it was like déjà vu from when I first took my physical for the department and had drunk so much to make the weight requirement; my bladder suddenly felt like it was going to explode.

Inside the office there were two plainclothes detectives. One was sitting behind a desk, and the other sat off to the side, just in my peripheral vision. They both had very grim expressions. I knew then that this wasn't going to be a good cop/bad cop sort of interview. This was LAPD Internal Affairs; it was going to be strictly bad cop/bad cop.

"Sit there," the one behind the desk said, gesturing to a chair on the other side.

Terrified, I sat down.

Pretty soon, the guy behind the desk pulled out an

8x10 head and shoulders shot of a guy dressed in a GI helmet and a GI peacoat. The peacoat was opened up, revealing a bare chest. The detective tossed the photo on the desk. I had never seen the guy in the photo before and I didn't recognize him, although I'll admit, he bore a passing resemblance to me. I only found out later that the picture was of John Holmes, a freakishly-endowed porn star.

"Is that you?" the guy behind the desk asked.

"No sir. That's not me."

"How can you be so sure?"

For some crazy reason, I came back with a sharp retort.

"Because I shaved this morning, and that's not the guy I saw in the mirror."

"Don't be a smart-ass Osmond, you're in big trouble here. Now why are you so sure that's not you? It kind of looks like you."

"Look," I said, "When I was in the movies, I was in the Confederate Army - I got killed. I got killed in another war movie by being run over by a car. I've been killed a number of times on the screen; but never as a US GI."

He paused for a second and his eyes bore right through me.

"Okay then. Let me get right to the point; how many adult films have you made Osmond?" He asked bluntly.

"What?" I said, incredulous.

"You heard me, tell us about it."

"I never have," I swore emphatically. "I was in regular movies and TV. I was Eddie Haskell. I never made an adult film. I don't even watch them."

He shuffled some papers around the desk, stalling, making me sweat even more –and I was sweating, even though I knew I had done nothing wrong. I had never made a porno film.

He went back and forth a number of times, rephrasing the question, trying to trip me up. I stayed resolute; I had never made a porno film and never would!

"Okay Osmond," he said finally. "You want to clear this whole thing up real quickly, you'll go along with us."

"What do you mean?"

"Stand up there and drop your pants."

"What?"

"You heard me. If you want to settle this right now, you'll drop your pants and show us what you've got."

I couldn't believe what I was hearing; a short arm inspection, *drop trou* right here in the hallowed halls of LAPD headquarters, Parker Center, a building named after a man who had come to the LAPD to clean it up. He was probably turning over in his grave right then.

But Parker couldn't help me, and I had no choice. There was no policeman's bill of rights at that time, and the union was a joke. Even though I had made it past my probation, these guys still had the power to run me out of the department. I was the family breadwinner and I had a wife, a child, and a big mortgage. I stood up and dropped my pants.

He took one glance and said, "Okay. You're free to go. Return to duty."

I was stunned; that was it? No explanation, no apology, just drop your pants and get back to work?

I pulled my pants back up and zipped them up. I turned to leave and then stopped and looked back at them, still in shock over what had happened.

"Why didn't you just put me on the polygraph machine?" I asked.

The detective shrugged. "We just thought this would be simpler."

* * *

The word spread like wildfire throughout the department about what happened. Guys are pretty big gossips in general, and cops are the worst. And then of course, the ribbing started. This was nothing new to me, I had endured ribbing ever since the academy by being called Eddie Haskell. But now with the John Holmes thing, oh this just gave the guys a whole new batch of arrows in their quiver.

The worst of it was when I had to go home and tell my wife Sandy, who is a devout Christian. She was understandably shocked, dismayed, and angry. I promised her I would get to the bottom of the situation and clear everything up.

No thanks to the charming fellows in internal affairs, over next couple of days I finally found out what was happening.

The department had got word somehow that a former child star by the name of Ken Osmond was making porno films, and that same Ken Osmond now worked for the LAPD. In reality, the person who alerted the department could have even been some of the guys I worked with, men who I knew watched porno films. But this wasn't simply a case of mistaken identity I was to discover. I learned that the film's distributors had taken the word of John Holmes, who in addition to having a lengthy appendage, was also given to telling very tall tales. And one of the tales he spun was that he had earlier starred in the TV show *Leave It to Beaver* – as Eddie Haskell!

The distributor stupidly took Holmes at his word, and immediately began packaging the films with the credit reading; starring *Ken Osmond as Eddie Haskell*. This wasn't just that we looked somewhat similar, I was being named directly! I had to go on the defensive to clear my reputation. I went on a mission to find the films.

* * *

Before the dawn of the internet, the only place you could find this stuff was in porno shops, which meant I had to go into them. This was embarrassing to me because it was not the sort of place I was used to frequenting. Still, it was what I had to do if I was going to get the proof I needed.

And so, I located adult bookstores in the area, strolled in nonchalantly, and asked if they had a section for John Holmes. If they did, they would point it out and I would go searching for the damning evidence. This was a few years before VHS tapes came out, so the films were either 8mm or 16mm films, known as "loops" in the industry.

I checked and checked, coming up empty. Then one day I walked into a small porno shop in the Valley and there it was, big as life, the words "Ken Osmond as Eddie Haskell" on the front of a filthy porno film.

"You son of a bitch!" I said, not caring who heard me.

I made up my mind then and there that I was going to sue John Holmes for damaging my good name.

I purchased two films that day as evidence, and then continued my quest. When I had gotten about a half dozen of them, I figured that I had enough to take to an attorney.

At first, the attorney didn't think we had a case, until he saw the films and the distributors' names on packages. But the problem with filmmakers, and especially adult filmmakers, is that production companies come and go. They are created, make a few films, and then fold up their tent, leaving very little trail to pick up. Still, he persisted.

In the meantime, it didn't take long for the rumor to spread beyond the department, and to the world in general. Pretty soon, the word was out that Eddie Haskell had turned to doing porno.

I took a lot of ribbing from the guys in the department, and could generally deal with it, but Sandy really took a hit at the church where several people who had heard the rumor, and obviously believed it, told her that they would pray for her.

People generally love any juicy story of a celebrity who has fallen from grace, but in this case, probably even more so when you place it against the backdrop of the *Beaver*, and the Eddie character.

Since the show had ended in 1963, a lot had changed in America. JFK was assassinated just a couple of months after our last regular episode aired. Then the Vietnam War spun out of control and spawned widespread protests. There were race riots across the US, and civil unrest. In 1968 both RFK and MLK were assassinated. And in 1970, National Guard Troops fired on protestors in Kent State, killing four people.

In short, America had not only lost its innocence, it had gotten very cynical in the process. The TV image of the squeaky clean, nuclear family now seemed ridiculous, even insulting to many Americans. And one of the families that typified that sterile existence, was none other than the Cleavers of Mayfield. A tumultuous decade later, the show now seemed like a façade, the characters no more than cardboard cutouts. All of course except for one character; good old Edward Clark Haskell.

Eddie was the lone holdout on the show, the one who would call BS when he saw it. He would be the one to pull down Santa's Claus's beard, or rip open the curtain on the Wizard of Oz. And he would do this while screaming out, "It's fake! It's all fake, I tell you!"

In this way, Eddie was the natural choice from the show for the "Most Likely to Turn to Porn Award", and America ate it up. Besides the obvious titillation with the rumor, it was another technology, or lack thereof, at work.

Without the internet to fact check on Snopes or Google, a rumor had an extremely long half-life back then. It could persist for years and years with no simple way to check its validity, not that anyone really wanted to know the truth anyway.

For this reason, the story stayed alive for many, many years after I was initially hauled onto the carpet at Parker Center.

But a funny thing happened on the way to infamy, the fan mail that had dried up years earlier started to reappear. And I began to receive requests for autographs and photos.

Suddenly, Eddie Haskell was very popular again.

Eddie Haskell Trivia answer Chapter 21: Before the ubiquitous use of cell phones, the LAPD would use the old fashioned call boxes to avoid having information, such as tense hostage situations, broadcast over the air waves where it could be intercepted by the media, who were known to use police scanners.

Eddie Haskell Trivia Chapter 22: Although he appeared to have a good case for defamation of character, Ken Osmond never prevailed against the porn distributors. The case was rejected by the Los Angeles Superior Court and finally went all the way to the State of California Appeals Court where it was tossed out because he was a public figure and it was considered satirical. How long did this whole

process take?
Answer at end of Chapter 23

TWENTY-THREE
A NEW ASSIGNMENT, A NEW BABY, AND A NEW RUMOR

After several years on the police department, I was reassigned to the North Hollywood division. This had nothing to do with the whole John Holmes thing, and was just the natural reshuffling of resources and manpower. It was nice being back on my home turf where I grew up, as it made one aspect of my job a whole lot easier; I always knew where I was if I had to call for assistance.

I worked patrol in North Hollywood for several years and attained the rank of P-3, which was similar to a corporal in the military. I also was made a training officer.

I was glad for the promotion, because soon I would have another mouth to feed. Sandy had gotten pregnant again.

Our second son, Christian Scott Osmond was born on June 12, 1974. Unlike the first go around with Eric, I was able to get off without having to code myself as sick in order to be there. Another difference was that I was able to be in the delivery room with Sandy when she gave birth, which was really special to me.

At home with our son Eric, entertaining me in my cop hat.

After a short time, I was pulled out of patrol and assigned to vice. My stint there was supposed to be eighteen months, but I knew shortly after being assigned, that I didn't want to go the distance.

Vice may seem exciting on TV, but the reality is, it's far from it. All of the crimes you handle are misdemeanors, and they are ones that for the most part, no one really cares about, like prostitution or gambling. You also generally don't take any calls, you patrol around in an unmarked car, and either find crimes being committed, or even initiate them.

We got lots of prostitution busts this way. My partner and I would drive around in our undercover car and pick up hitchhikers. If they were young females hitchhiking by themselves, they would usually be pros. They'd climb into the car and after a short distance, would offer us sexual favors if we drove them all the way to such and such, or for some money. So we would bust them.

Another thing that gets busted a lot in vice, is your own butt. You'd find a guy in a park restroom, soliciting for homosexual favors or exposing himself, and you'd ID yourself and attempt to arrest him. And boy would those guys fight you like no one's business.

You'd find out after you booked them that the guy had worked for Lockheed for twenty years, had a wife and a family, and went to church every Sunday. He'd fight you every step of the way, because he'd rather be arrested for bank robbery, than for what you were busting him for.

I really hated vice and didn't feel it was a good fit for me. After a couple of months, I asked my supervisor if there was any way to be taken off of it and put back on patrol. He thought that he could swing it so I thanked him and left.

I was walking down the hall the day after talking to my supervisor, when another cop yelled out, "Hey, Eddie?"

I turned toward him, thinking it was going to be another John Holmes joke. Instead, he said, "So I hear you're Alice Cooper now."

* * *

Alice Cooper,
"When people asked me what I was like as a kid, I would say I was like a 'regular' Eddie Haskell, meaning that's the type of kid I was. Of course I was really nothing like that, but it was such a cool reference, I said it. But the press interpreted the statement, as I WAS the real Eddie Haskell!"

Although it was another outrageous rumor, I was getting used to them and wasn't offended by it like I was with the John Holmes thing. I didn't hold with people thinking I was the *King of Porn*, but it didn't faze me too much for people to think I was the *Godfather of Shock-*

Rock. I also didn't have to go to internal affairs again and prove that I wasn't Alice Cooper by singing. Just like the Holmes thing, that investigation would have been settled very quickly!

So now at thirty years old, I had two children, and two rumors chasing me. Actually, Alice Cooper had the rumor chasing him as well.

> *Alice Cooper,*
> *"The whole Eddie Haskell thing reminded me of the*
> *"biting off the head of a live chicken thing" in*
> *Toronto. It was one of those things that people latch*
> *onto as an urban legend that we could not get rid*
> *of."*

Alice Cooper eventually grew so tired of being asked if he was Eddie Haskell, he finally had a T-shirt made that read, "NO. I AM NOT EDDIE HASKELL."

Permission to use image courtesy Alice Cooper.
Alice apparently grew tired of rumors as well.

Around 1975, I applied for motors, meaning riding a motorcycle as a police officer. It was considered a plumb position if you were going to be in a blue suit. A couple of months later, I was accepted and told to report to the motorcycle officer training school. It was a three week long school, and was located down in Terminal Island, which was quite a commute, so a bunch of us who were accepted to the school carpooled from San Fernando Valley.

Every day we had to wear boots, a long sleeve shirt, and gloves for when we crashed, which I didn't think I would be doing.

It has been a widely circulated story that a lot of the people I arrested recognized me and thought it was "cool" getting busted by Eddie Haskell. In reality, very few people recognized me when I was a cop.

I had been riding motorcycles ever since Dayton and I had had pushed our Cushman Scooter home twenty-two years ago, and I thought they weren't going to teach me anything about how to ride a bike. Boy, did they turn that theory on its head. These guys were great instructors!

I learned things I never knew were possible to do with a motorcycle. Like how to get a motorcycle up if it's on its side. You don't pick it up, but you ride it up with you on it!

When I first heard that I thought, "No way; you don't ride a 900-pound Harley Davidson up from the ground!" But they proved me wrong, and taught me how to do it.

They also taught us how to turn a motorcycle around 180 degrees without leaving a lane *and* how to back up a motorcycle without pushing it. And no, they didn't have reverse gears.

I was amazed that I knew so little about riding a bike.

Getting into motors opened up a whole new vista of police work for me to learn and explore. It also brought me back once again to the industry that I couldn't seem to escape, no matter where I went or what I was doing.

By being in motors, I got to work security for the entertainment industry.

* * *

Outdoor television and movie sets have their own unique sets of problems; there are lighting issues, weather, and background noise. Most of these issues, the studios have no control over, but crowd control and access to the shoot was something that was within their sphere of influence – especially when they used motor officers.

On a cycle you are highly mobile and can get from one place to another very quickly. We would be used for traffic control, blocking off intersections, following cars in chase scenes, and similar duties. It was easy work and paid very well, something very important to me with two growing boys in the house.

I worked on TV shows like *Baretta* and *Barnaby Jones*. One time, the star of the show, Buddy Ebsen, actually came to my rescue.

It had started to rain, and the cast and crew had to wait it out until we could resume shooting. All of the crew members were holed up underneath a canopy, but we were expected to remain on sentry duty. I was sitting on my bike in the pouring rain when the door to a very nice motor home opened up and a hand stuck out, gesturing me inside.

"C'mon," he said. "Get in here. They ain't doing any shoot'n out there."

"Thanks."

I stepped inside and there he was; Jed Clampett himself. He was becoming a household name in America at about the same time that *Leave it Beaver* was going into syndication.

But we didn't talk about the old times of television work. There was more serious business to attend to.

"You look pretty soaked there Officer Osmond," he observed.

"Yes sir."

"And I bet you could use a drink."

"Yes sir."

And so, he pulled out a bottle of Jack Daniels and a couple of glasses. And then America's *poor mountaineer* and *preeminent bad boy* shared a drink.

I did plenty of feature films too. And on one of those, I actually got fired for being a cop and doing my job.

It was called *Car Wash* and was considered a "blaxploitation" film, even though it had a multi-racial cast. During one of the breaks, some of the film crew started up a craps game on the set. Even though it was on their set, it was still against the law and we were still sworn peace officers in uniform. It would not look good if someone saw a bunch of cops standing by idly while the law was being broken. So we asked them, "Hey guys, you think you could take it inside or something? We could get in trouble here if someone sees us."

One of them looked up from the game and very loudly suggested an anatomical impossibility. Then they had us fired and thrown off the set.

And then there were the just plain crazy times.

We were working in downtown Los Angeles, near an area known as skid row for its huge homeless population. We were in between scenes and had the movie car sitting by the curb with the door open. A drunk wandered by and he got in, started it up, and took off. We had to chase him down and arrest him – right there on the set!

* * *

Around this time on motors, I ended up getting assigned to deuce patrol, which is what the department called drunk driving patrol. I think for most cops it's generally considered a punitive sort of assignment because it has crappy hours as you're working almost exclusively at night. But I really enjoyed it and thought that it was the best assignment I could have been given. It was also where I met some of the best cops I had ever worked with, and we had a real brotherhood. I'm still very close with most of them to this day.

Our location to patrol couldn't have made for easier pickings. We were in the Rampart Division around MacArthur Park, a high crime, heavy substance abuse area. It was such a target rich environment that we had a pretty high quota we were expected to fill. Even with it though, we had little trouble making our numbers. After we would spot a suspected drunk driver, we would pull him over on our bikes and give him the field sobriety test. If he failed, and almost all of the ones we pulled over did, we would have them transported to the station for booking. Since we couldn't put the suspect on our bikes, we had a van that picked them up for us. It was so easy to catch them there, on one night, my partner Henry Lane and I got seven DUI's in thirty-five minutes!

My good partner Henry Lane and I pose with Eileen Anderson, who was a fixture downtown. She would wear these crazy outfits and protest (peacefully) in front of city hall. She ran for LA Mayor one time, and I actually voted for her.

But as much as I loved the guys I worked with, like a

lot of cops, I had become somewhat jaded after starting out with lofty goals of what I would be able to accomplish.

> *Sandy Osmond,*
> *"Ken was one of the cops that was going to change the world, he thought."*

The system of justice seemed like a revolving door, with more rights for the criminals than for the people who obeyed the law. Sometimes you'd see the same guy you busted back on the streets in just a day or so. One night, I even busted the same guy for drunk driving *twice* during the same shift. I had busted him at the beginning of the shift, and before I got off, I saw his friend, who had obviously bailed him out, drop him off at his car. So I pulled him over, gave him the test, and he failed again.

After several years of seeing this, I started feeling like I was just spinning my wheels. It seemed like I wasn't making a difference to anybody in the world

...except for one person.

> *Eddie Haskell Trivia answer Chapter 22: It took over eleven years for Ken Osmond's lawsuit against the pornographers that had used his name to finally settle, unsuccessfully. And it all ended very unceremoniously. His attorney called to deliver the bad news from the appellate court. "We lost," he said. "It's over Ken."*

> *Eddie Haskell Trivia Chapter 23: Ken Osmond once turned the tables and pulled off a little "shock" himself on Alice Cooper. What did he do? Answer at the end of Chapter 24*

TWENTY-FOUR
KIM RODERICK

Kim Roderick,
"I was really glad that Ken and his partner Henry
would look after me, because no one else was
around. I needed normalcy, and Kenny was the
most normal thing in my life."

She was just a young, innocent girl, who had all the cards stacked against her. In 1970, her mom moved Kim and her brother down from Toronto, Canada. They had no place to stay, no green cards, and only 27 cents combined in their pockets. Even when they got to LA, they moved constantly, at least three times a year. It was very rough on her.

Henry and I met her around 1977, when she was working as a hostess at a restaurant on our beat named Jerry's. Cops ate for half price there and the food was good, but that wasn't the only reason we went there.

Kim Roderick,
"I was just a naïve kid from Canada, who had

*never even seen a homeless person before I came
here. I had some of the worst, most frightening
experiences in LA, and between my boss, Jerry and
those two (Ken and Henry), they looked out for me.
It was also the time of the 'Hillside Strangler,' who
were actually two men that went on a raping and
killing rampage in 1977-78."*

I guess you could say that we pretty much "adopted"
Kim from the two deuce cops who came before us,
which was fine with us. She had been working at Jerry's
for about a year or so before we came on the scene.
Because her mother was working several jobs, she was a
latchkey kid with no place to go. She was having a cup
of coffee in Jerry's one day, when the owner was curious
about why a fourteen-year-old girl was sitting in the
restaurant without a parent. She told him that she didn't
have anywhere to go and asked for a job, so he hired her
on the spot.

Henry and I would come in and have dinner there.
We were supposed to get forty-five minutes for our meal
break, but it usually stretched out to a lot longer.

Kim Roderick,
*"I knew that the guys were supposed to get forty-
five minutes for their meal, but they would just keep
hanging out longer and longer. It would easily
stretch to an hour and half, and sometimes two
hours. Kenny was the conscientious one and would
keep saying to Henry, 'We should get back to
patrol.' And Henry would fire back, 'Don't worry,
no one's drinking yet. We can wait; we'll still get
our quota.'"*

I honestly don't know what we talked about, but I
guess we did a lot of it. Henry and I were always

concerned about her well-being and would find out if anyone was bothering her and how she was doing. We taught her how to be aware of her surroundings, and we even got her a can of mace and trained her how to use it. It came in handy for her one night when she was walking to work.

> Kim Roderick,
> "I heard footsteps behind me and turned to see a naked man following me. Just like Kenny and Henry had taught me to always keep my hand on the mace can, I was ready, and pulled it out and sprayed him. Kenny and Henry took down a report and before long I think every cop in the Rampart Division was looking for this guy."

After Kim's incident, we began riding her route every time we went on patrol. We rode it before she began work, and before she got off work. If she was opening the restaurant in the morning, we would make sure there was a patrol car sitting in the parking lot, watching to make sure she got in okay. It was team effort in a lot of ways. Although, a lot of times Kim had to wonder how Henry and I made a team.

> Kim Roderick,
> "Henry was always throwing Kenny under the bus, including telling me about the John Holmes incident. Henry even brought in a porno magazine one night and said, laughing, 'Doesn't that look like Kenny in a wig?' Kenny was so pissed off, especially because he's so strait-laced and conservative. If anyone was going to get in trouble, it would be Henry!"

But I got back at Henry, actually Kim and I both did.

Her mom moved back up to Canada at one point, and convinced Kim to move back up with her. She moved up there and stayed about a year. But it was tough on Kim; she couldn't make much money, and the guy her mom was seeing was an alcoholic. She would write back to Henry and me and tell us about how bad it was, and how she missed being out here. I would always write Kim back, but Henry would not.

She called one day to tell me that she was moving back...*and* that she was ticked off at Henry for not writing! And so we concocted a plan to throw a pie in Henry's face at role call one day.

> *Kim Roderick,*
> *"I got a graham cracker pie crust and I wanted to fill it with whipped cream. But Kenny knew from his time in the movies and TV, that you had to use shaving cream, because the oil in the whip cream would stain clothing, and we didn't want to ruin Henry's uniform."*

That day I snuck Kim into headquarters with the shaving cream pie. Then I went into the squad room for role call, making sure that Henry and I were seated in front row. Everybody was in on the joke, except for Henry of course. Then Kim came into the squad room and pushed the pie, shaving cream and all, into Henry's face screaming, "Why didn't you ever write me Henry?!"

Of course, then all of the cops starting cracking up. Henry sat there stunned for a second, and then he started laughing himself. He laughed so hard he couldn't stop.

Kim and I really got back at Henry.

One thing we hadn't figured on though was the graham cracker crust. The shaving cream wiped off fine, but there were crumbs stuck all over his uniform shirt. Finally, after we realized it was hopeless to try to pick them off, I went into the locker room and "borrowed," another shirt from a fellow officer.

We had lots of fun with Kim, even when we were looking out for her. But sometimes she thought we took things a little too far. Like when she started to date and we'd run the plates of the guys taking her out.

Kim Roderick,
"I was on a date one evening and in the guy's car and we were driving down the boulevard on our way to dinner. Before I knew it, there were flashing lights behind us. My date, stunned, didn't know what he did, but he pulled over. And then I see that it's Kenny and Henry on their bikes. So I told my date, 'Don't worry, I know these guys.'

So I went back to talk to them, and in the meantime,

they're jacking my date up, giving him the real third degree. I got back into the car with my date and he's sitting there staring straight ahead, his hands holding the wheel in a death-grip. I tell him not to worry about it, and to forget about Kenny and Henry.

He took me to dinner, took me straight home, and couldn't get away from me fast enough. At times I thought I was going to turn out to be an old maid because of Kenny and Henry!"

Henry and I had lots of memorable times in Jerry's eating and talking with Kim. But none were as memorable as one particular Saturday evening. The place was busy that night, with us cops on one side of the restaurant, and the local Korean Mafia on the other. Kim, as usual, was hustling tables and trading wisecracks with Henry and me. To me, it was just like a million other nights I had spent in there.

Except that night, in just a couple of hours, I would be flat on my back on the sidewalk, paralyzed. I would have taken three rounds at point blank range, and the shooter, a convicted murderer, would have his gun to my head to finish me off. It was September 20, 1980.

Eddie Haskell Trivia answer Chapter 23: Hearing that Alice Cooper was in Los Angeles and rehearsing for his "Welcome To My Nightmare" show, Officer Ken Osmond decide to pull a little "shock-rock" of his own. He showed up on the set in his uniform and very formally asked to speak to Alice Cooper. When a very nervous Alice Cooper came out a few minutes later, Ken took off his helmet and glasses and said, "Hi Alice, I'm the real Eddie Haskell."

Eddie Haskell Trivia Chapter 24: Besides giving Kenny and Henry fits by going out on dates, Kim Roderick earned their ire when she was part of a production for a police training film. The location for the film was at a fraternity house where a lot of the rookie cops lived. Lots of drinking and carrying on was a regular occurrence at the house. The house was the setting for a famous novel by an LAPD officer-turned-novelist. What was the name of the book and who was its author?
Answer at the end of Chapter 25

TWENTY-FIVE
RECOVERY, AND DEJA-VU

September 20, 1980

After the hospital personnel patched up my wounds and determined that they were not life threatening, I asked for a phone to call home. One of the things you learn as a cop is that if something happens to you: you are shot, crash...whatever, you *never* have someone else call home for you if you are able to do it yourself. The wife of a cop lives in constant fear for her husband, and any phone call, especially one that comes in the middle of the night, is one of the things they dread most. And to hear another cop's voice on the other end only makes matters worse.

I called Sandy and the first words I said to her was that there had been an incident and that I was all right. She asked what happened and I told her that I had been shot, but that I was fine.

Sandy Osmond,
"I remember that after Ken called, the first thing I

*did was go into our sons' bedroom and looked at
Eric and Christian in bed. I thought, 'Their dad
could be gone right now.'"*

*"I needed to talk to somebody so I wouldn't go
crazy, but I didn't want to tell my parents, and so I
called a friend of ours and a fellow officer by the
name of Suni (pronounced Sunny). I guess I figured
that being a female, and a fellow cop, she would
understand. My assumption was correct and she
came right over, we made a pot of coffee, and she
kept me occupied until Ken finally got home. We
talked about all kinds of stuff through the wee hours
of the morning - anything except police work."*

About seven o'clock in the morning, my supervisor
dropped me off at home along with my pain meds,
which I would really need over the next couple of weeks.

While body armor will stop certain rounds from
penetrating and striking vital organs, it still can't stop the
massive amount of blunt force trauma that a bullet
carries with it. A .38 caliber bullet weighs only 7 grams,
or less than a quarter of an ounce, but at the speed that
it's travelling, it can deliver over 300 pounds of force,
especially at point blank range. It's like getting hit with a
sledgehammer!

*Christian Osmond,
"One of the things I remember about the shooting
was seeing Dad all bandaged up and kind of
stumbling down the hallway at our house. I still
have that vision in my head."*

Ironically, the wound that could have been the most
lethal, the one that hit the belt buckle, didn't really hurt.
The one where the bullet struck my vest in the lower left

hurt a little bit. But the upper right chest wound, the one right by my breastbone, hurt like crazy! Even though the vest stopped full penetration, I had a scar, and my right chest and right arm turned completely black and blue. Besides being in pain and bruised, my right arm was completely useless to me and I had to keep it in a sling.

I was coded as IOD, or Injury On Duty, and could only return to work when the doctor said so, not when I felt like it. I saw the physician a couple of times during the first month and eventually, my pain began to diminish. After a couple of weeks, my arm felt better and I could use it again. That was good, because two weeks after the shooting Henry threw a party at his house for me. It was sort of a, *We're glad to see you're okay Ken*, type of affair, and a lot of the deuce guys were there that I had worked with. It was very special to me and reminded me that I was truly part of a brotherhood. These guys were really special, and were very supportive throughout my whole ordeal.

After being off for about a month, the doctor deemed me well enough to go back to work, but only on light duty. I was assigned to a desk and did reports, filing, and other such tasks. My guess is that the department wants to ease people back into the job slowly, especially after being subjected to such a traumatic event such as being shot.

Thanks to TV, lots of people have a skewed idea about police work and they think that officers get shot all the time. Maybe it's more common now, but back in the '70s and '80s it was somewhat rare. In fact, in the entire time I was at the LAPD, I only knew one other cop who had been shot. I met him at the academy and he had a bullet graze the top of his hand. I'm sure there were others in the department that I didn't know about, but he was the only one I ever met in all my years as an officer.

Two months after the shooting, I was deemed fit to

return to regular patrol. It was great being with Henry again, but I can't say I was that thrilled to return to the mean streets of Rampart Division. Normally, you work alone on motors until the sun goes down, then you team up with your partner for the rest of your shift during the night. But I found that I wanted to stick by Henry through my whole shift, light or dark. I guess being around him added to a sense of security for me after what happened.

But even sticking close by Henry couldn't save me from the terror of what happened next, because just two and half months after my shooting, it happened again.

Eddie Haskell Trivia answer Chapter 24: The location for the film that Kim made at the fraternity house was used as the backdrop for the book "The Choirboys" by LAPD officer turned best-selling-novelist, Joseph Waumbaugh.

Eddie Haskell Trivia Chapter 25: Besides being a close family friend, Suni eventually became a part of Sandy and Ken's extended family when she did what?
Answer at the end of Chapter 26

TWENTY-SIX
POST TRAUMATIC STRESS DISORDER

Henry and I were working one evening and we had pulled over a DUI suspect at the intersection of Wilshire Boulevard and Alvarado Street near MacArthur Park. After the guy failed the field sobriety test, we arrested and cuffed him, and called for our transport van to bring him into the station.

While we were waiting for the van to show up, we saw a guy running right up the middle of Alvarado, which was a little odd. I ran out into the street and tried to stop him, and he turned and headed into the park. "Well," I thought. "If he doesn't want to talk to me, I definitely want to talk to him." So I chased up after him.

He circled through the park and then came back out, and cut diagonally across the intersection of the street and went into an alley.

Henry saw what was going on and cuffed our DUI to the crash-bar on his motorcycle, and began to chase the suspect with me. I didn't know that Henry was behind me, and neither of us knew that a private security guard, who was armed with a .357 Magnum, was also chasing the suspect. I felt it before I heard it.

The .357 round is supersonic, which means it will fly faster than the speed of sound. When I was about halfway down the alley in pursuit of the suspect, a bullet came right by the side of my head, over my ear. It literally parted my hair above my ear. Then I heard the distinctive boom when the sound caught up to me, and I knew what was happening. I was being shot at – again!

I stopped in my tracks, sat down, and promptly threw up.

* * *

Henry screamed at the security guard not to fire, and continued chasing down the suspect. He caught the suspect at the end of the alley. I was still shaking and physically ill.

Pretty soon, the whole scene was crawling with cops. As soon as I saw that Henry was okay, I went and sat down again. My supervisor, a great guy by the name of Dick Stoddard, came over to check on me.

"You okay Ken?" he asked.

I shook my head. "I'm going to get some coffee," I said.

I took off on my bike and drove a couple of blocks to a donut shop we used to frequent. I got a coffee and stood there, drinking it.

After a few minutes, Dick rode up in the squad car to see if I was doing okay.

As soon as I saw him, I said, "I'm going home Dick. And I don't care how you code me."

He said, "Don't worry, it's covered."

And so I got on my motorcycle and rode home. It was the beginning of a long period when I didn't care about anything.

* * *

Although my physical wounds were immediate, and healed rather quickly, the emotional trauma I suffered progressed at a slower rate, creeping into my life. Before long, I was profoundly depressed, I couldn't sleep at night, and I didn't care at all about anything.

I stopped seeing my friends and I didn't want to talk to anyone, including Sandy and my own two sons. I would get up before my shift and like a zombie, go into work and do my duty, all without really thinking about it or caring about it. Later, when I got home, I would head straight into the den, and lock the door behind me. I would be in there for two to three days at a time.

Sandy Osmond,
"It came very close to ending our marriage. He just wouldn't talk. I told my mom, 'I don't think I can do this any longer.' She assured me that it would pass. I wasn't so sure about it, and neither was Ken."

Sandy finally decided to go to the department and get me some help. There were six *full time* shrinks at LAPD. What does *that* tell you about the stress a cop is under? They assigned one to me and I began to go see him.

The first thing he did of course was to prescribe pills, which I wasn't crazy about, but I went along with the program. However, the pills had some bizarre side effects, and I really didn't think they were doing me a whole lot of good. So I stopped taking them and asked to see another shrink. This one put me on medical leave and had me seeing him regularly. Being away from the stress of the job helped, but things were getting even worse at home.

I would start crying for no reason, finding myself welling up and crying, and not knowing why. It could happen anywhere, anytime, and for no reason whatsoever. And then there were the nightmares.

Sandy Osmond,
"Ken would wake up in a complete panic, sweating,
and thrashing about. And the nightmares were
getting more intense, and more frequent. He was
completely exhausted because he wasn't sleeping.
He didn't like himself. He didn't like being asleep,
and he didn't like being awake. I was really worried
that he would become suicidal."

Up to this point, I didn't have suicidal thoughts, but I think I would have gotten to them if something weren't done to help me.

I started bouncing around different shrinks in the department. Then they would think I was fine and put me back on regular duty. But I wasn't fine, not at home, and not at work.

I noticed that I was shying away from doing things in the field that I would have done before, like taking police action. Before the shootings, if I found a carload of gang-bangers, I would pull 'em over and see what was going on, but after, I was avoiding it. And I didn't know if it was fear, or just plain apathy. I also didn't even care if I showed up for work or not.

Up until that point in my career, I had never taken a sick day in the ten years I had been on the police department. After the second shooting, I found myself taking sick days regularly. It even got to the point where I would get dressed in my uniform, get onto the motorcycle, and then just say, "Screw it!" I'd put it back on the kickstand, go into the house, and call in sick.

Finally, after a year or so of torment, and a bunch of shrinks, I found my savior.

* * *

Her name was Liliane Quon McCain. She was a

second generation Chinese-American, and she saved my life.

I would go to her house in Beverly Hills. She had a completely finished basement with a fireplace, and it was very cozy and inviting. We would go down into basement and we would just talk – about anything

I really clicked with her. I think that's the most important thing about seeing someone like that, is to "click."

I saw Liliane for three years, even after I thought I was cured. Every once in a while, I would feel a depression coming on, and I would call her up and see her. She helped me get through it.

From my experiences, I know that PTSD is a very real thing. I sympathize with GI's, knowing that many of them have experienced far more than I had. And I would like to tell them one thing,

"You can get through it. If I can get through it, you can too. I don't need a shrink now, but I did then. The secret is to finding a shrink you can click with. I know because I went through thirteen of them before I found the one that saved my life."

Eddie Haskell Trivia answer Chapter 25: Suni eventually became a part of Sandy and Ken's extended family when she married Sandy's brother, Vance.

Eddie Haskell Trivia Chapter 26: Eric and Christian Osmond would sometimes accompany their dad to Liliane's home in Beverly Hills to swim in her pool. There was one very unique feature of the house that they enjoyed as well. What was it? Answer at the end of Chapter 27

TWENTY-SEVEN
1982, BACK TO UNIVERSAL

Ever since the original *Leave It to Beaver* was cancelled in 1963, a small but dedicated cadre of fans had been clamoring for its return to the airways in the form of a revival show. Occasionally, these voices would be heard somewhere in Tinsel Town, and a seed would be planted. The seed would take root, germinate, and grow rapidly. But just as quickly though, it would become neglected and forgotten, only to die on the vine and wither away to memory.

This scenario had played itself out many times in the two-decade hiatus from the show and all of us – Barbara, Hugh, Jerry, Tony, Frank, and I - had seen many false starts. I had given up any hope that a revival show would ever be made. Promises to the contrary were given the same credence by me as an Elvis sighting, nice to think it was true, but it probably wasn't.

So when television producer and writer, Brian Levant contacted me in 1981 about a revival show, I was polite and expressed my interest in doing a show. But I wasn't about to start holding my breath waiting for it to come to fruition.

However, Brian wasn't your garden-variety producer in an industry that had more than its share; he was a seasoned pro who had an impressive resume of shows such as *Mork and Mindy* and *Happy Days*. In other words, Brian had the chops. More than that, as a rabid *Beaver* fan, he had the passion as well.

> *Brian Levant,*
> *"I remember seeing the first show when I was five years old and I loved it! It was a reflection of my own life because I was an older brother with a goofy younger brother named 'Guffy.' Leave It to Beaver really resonated with me."*

But passion only takes you so far in this business, and Brian still had to navigate the Byzantine world of Hollywood's power brokers to eventually spot the elusive green light in the distance. After teaming up with fellow producer Nick Abdo, of *Happy Days* and *Laverne and Shirley* fame, a shape began to emerge in the fog. The shape was a movie of the week, or MOW, that was to be a pilot show for a new series titled *Still The Beaver*.

* * *

Maybe the voices that had been crying for the show to return had finally been heard, or maybe it was the fact that after the turbulent '60s and '70s, America was finally ready for a little peace and quiet with some familiar faces in good old Mayfield. Either way, we were moving forward with something that I never thought I would see in my life again.

The initial plan for the show was to reunite the entire original cast, and some of its many guest stars, and return us to the mythical town of present day Mayfield. As the times had changed substantially since 1963, and we were obviously adults now – with adult type problems, the show would have some twists and turns. Beaver was to become estranged from his wife after she follows her dream to become a veterinarian and moves out of the country. The Beaver is left to raise their two sons; Corey, played by Corey Feldman, and Oliver, played by John Snee. He has no job and must move back in with his mother June to their old home at 211 Pine Street. He takes a job with the Rutherford firm, still run by Fred Rutherford, who is now "ably" assisted by his now fully-grown, but still whiney son Clarence (Lumpy).

Wally, in the meantime, still lives in Mayfield and is a successful attorney. He's married to his high school sweetheart Mary Ellen Rogers, played by Janice Kent. Wally and his wife want for nothing in this world, except a child, which they have been trying desperately to have as Wally is struggling with impotence. They also would like to have some newer, bigger digs, and that's where the good old neighborhood nemesis, Eddie Haskell comes in.

After a fashion, Eddie finally landed in a job he can handle. He's the proud owner of Haskell Construction Company where the motto is, "Building a Better Mayfield." *Owner* is a rather nebulous term here though, as Eddie's business is in receivership and he has everyone from suppliers, to subcontractors, to the IRS after him. His wife was even the one who turned him in to the IRS!

Acting as his pro bono attorney, Wally has managed to keep his dubious friend's butt out of jail for the time being, but even this counselor has his limits as Eddie tries his patience. Eddie attempts to repay his legal debt to his friend by building a new "dream home" for Wally and his wife. But in typical Eddie fashion, he's continually overrunning the budget, missing deadlines, or getting caught using substandard materials. In fact, in one of the first scenes of the movie, Wally delivers a two decade's overdue punch to the belly of his "best friend" Eddie.

While the plan had been to reunite the entire crew, one member was noticeably absent. Hugh Beaumont had suffered a severe stroke several years earlier, and as much as he would have liked to have been involved, he declined due to health reasons. The script was changed to show him as deceased. He passed away on May 14, 1982. It was the same day the final script had been finished for the movie.

*   *   *

Since this was 1981, all of this was taking place against the backdrop of my mental health troubles. Since I had met Liliane, my deep depression had waned, but I was still suffering from intense job burnout. My condition didn't escape the attention of my superiors, and I was continually bouncing back and forth from being put on medical leave, and then returned to active duty. To be back on the *Beaver* set playing Eddie again was a welcome respite. Acting was natural to me, and it was the one time I could escape into a different being for some time.

Sandy, Christian, Eric and myself on the Universal set for the movie of the week.

Another great thing about doing *Still The Beaver* was that I could act with my son Eric, who would play my son *Eddie Jr.* on the show. In all my years in show business, and all of my years raising my children, it was something that I had never dreamed possible.

Brain Levant,
"When we started getting close to pulling the whole
thing together, I had told Ken, 'Hey, we're looking
for someone to play your son on the show. And your
son Eric is about the right age, have him audition."

I asked Eric about it and he was game to give it a try. But he wasn't just going to waltz into it unprepared. Even at a young age, Eric always wanted to learn every aspect of something before he tackled it. He and I would sit for hours and watch the tapes I had made of the original program so that he could study Eddie's every mannerism and tic. I even served as his dialogue coach to hone his rendition of the famous, *Heh, heh, heh* "Eddie cackle."

But coaching Eric on dialogue at home was one thing, being on the set with him was another. The director is king on the set, and he would be the one to instruct Eric once we got on to the sound stage. I had seen too many stage parents through the years trying to second guess a director, and I knew how destructive it could be. On the set, Eric Osmond was just a fellow actor, and nothing more.

* * *

We began shooting the movie in the fall of 1982. I had to take some of my vacation time from LAPD in order to swing it. Even though the bulk of the show was shot at Universal, the first day of shooting was on location in Sand Canyon, a sparsely developed area north of Los Angeles. It was to serve as the fictional site of Wally and Mary Ellen's dream home as it was being built by Haskell Construction. In the scene, I came flying onto the property in my work truck and knocked down a sign. Wally and his wife Mary Ellen were hot on my trail in his classic T-Bird and they chased me down and cornered me. Wally's was so fed up with my antics, he gut punched me. It was the punch fans had been telling Wally to throw for decades.

What was amazing was that we did no formal rehearsals prior to shooting, and no table reads. We just showed up to the set, rehearsed our lines a couple of times, blocked them, and then started shooting. We were all older, but it was like those two decades had never even passed; time had stood still. We just kind of picked up where we left off. It all felt very natural to me and didn't seem like work at all.

> *Sandy Osmond,*
> *"Watching Ken in the movie of the week, it was like Eddie never went away, even after twenty years. He was still the old Eddie. Nobody had to re-train him for the part he did as a kid."*

Acting again and playing Eddie was very therapeutic for me, and it was definitely fun for my son Eric to be on the set for the production.

> *Eric Osmond,*
> *"I remember that there was a scene being shot at the LA zoo. And the driver would pick you up and take us out to the zoo, and we didn't have to pay to get in, and they had donuts and everything. Being a little kid, I thought that was really cool."*

Besides the old cast, even a lot of the original crew from the first series were brought in to work on *Still The Beaver*. So it was like going home in a lot of ways. One of these fixtures I saw was old Scotty, whose real name was William McGlynn. He was the gate guard at Universal and had worked there for decades, including when I was doing the original show. Everybody who worked in the industry at Universal knew Scotty. After not having stepped foot onto the Universal lot for so long, it was real pleasure to see his familiar face.

The movie we shot, like many, was produced as a vehicle to sell a series to the networks. It was used to establish baseline characters and situations, such as Beaver's struggles as a single parent, Tony and Mary Ellen's desire for children, June's thrill at being a doting grandmother, and of course, Eddie's perpetual cageyness – which he has now passed on in his DNA to Eddie Jr.

And since *Still The Beaver* was created to hopefully sell a revival series, a lot of footage from the original show had been cut in with the new scenes. But it wasn't gratuitous cuts just to show how much we had grown in twenty years; the director used scenes that mirrored what was happening in the movie. For example, when Beaver is having trouble gaining respect from his own sons, he flashes back painfully to the memory of Ward reading the glowing essay Beaver had written for school about how his dad was the most interesting person he knew. In the movie, when Beaver and Wally get into a big argument in front of Lumpy and Eddie, the scene cuts to an original show that showed them fighting as brothers. This is also a scene in the revival show where the old Eddie comes out:

LUMPY
(Trying to get Wally and Beaver to make peace)
"C'mon you guys. Break it up and let's talk about it."

EDDIE
(To LUMPY)
"What are you Lump, the U.N.? I want to see some fur fly!"

My own relationship with my son Eddie Jr. was somewhat vague in the movie as we only had one scene together. In it, Beaver's son Corey, and Eddie Jr. both get caught doing some graffiti at their elementary school and are sent to the principal's office. When Eddie Jr. is released to the custody of his father, the younger Haskell reacts with typical obsequiousness.

EDDIE JR.
"Good afternoon Dad. There seems to be a case of mistaken identity here."

EDDIE
(Grabbing Eddie Jr. by the shirt collar and hauling him off)
"C'mon you little fella! When I get done with you, you're going to be stamping license plates for go-karts!"

We never know in the movie if Eddie is really trying to play the stern role model to his child, or if he's just putting on an act in front of the principle. One thing was crystal clear though, Eddie Jr. was a chip off the old block.

* * *

We were budgeted with nineteen days to shoot the movie, and we wrapped it in seventeen, which pleased the production company to no end. And then we had a wrap party, which was a lot of fun, with plenty of drinking, laughing and carrying on.

Finally, after a twenty-year dearth of new *Beaver* episodes, the movie of the week, *Still The Beaver* debuted on March 19, 1983. It had huge ratings in the last half-hour, with 6 out of 8 overnight markets reporting a 50% share. The overall share was 38%, which made it the second highest rated MOW that year. Part of the reason for this was that it appealed to what's known in the industry as a bimodal audience; baby-boomers who had grown up with the original show, watched the revival show with their children or grandchildren.

We did the same thing when *Still The Beaver* premiered, and watched it with the whole family. We had a great big screening party at our house. Even my cop friends showed up to razz me.

With the movie out and with such high ratings, we felt sure it was a given that a series was going to get made. The studio had an option for eighteen months before they had to exercise it or move on, and they held us out for *entire eighteen* months. Finally, in July of 1984, we got the call. The series was a go. According to the Brian Levant, the character of Eddie was instrumental in selling the series.

> *Brian Levant,*
> *"Eddie Haskell made the show. Without Eddie, it was like eating bland food compared to spiced food. I don't think we could have sold the show without Eddie."*

* * *

Eddie Haskell Trivia answer Chapter 26: When Eric and Christian Osmond accompanied their dad to Liliane's home in Beverly Hills, they would enjoy playing in the secret tunnel that went from the kitchen to the office. You entered it by moving a fake wall.

Eddie Haskell Trivia Chapter 27: In the MOW, there was a subtle homage, sometimes known as an

"Easter Egg" in industry parlance, to a person who was very influential in Ken Osmond's development as the character Eddie Haskell. Who was that person?
Answer at the end of Chapter 28

TWENTY-EIGHT
1984-89
THE SERIES: THE NEW LEAVE IT TO BEAVER

After holding our collective breaths for so long, the series was finally picked up and we got an order for thirty episodes from the Disney Channel. All of us were ready to get right to work, but nothing ever stays the same in Hollywood and there were some significant changes being made. For one, actor Corey Feldman, who played the Beaver's son Corey in the movie, would be replaced with Kipp Marcus, a veteran Broadway actor, who would go by the character name, Ward "Kip" Cleaver. Beaver's son Oliver would remain in the script, and would continued to be played by the very capable, John Snee.

Also, Tony's impotence in the MOW magically disappears, and he and Mary Ellen were now blessed with a cute eight-year-old daughter. Her name would be Kelly Cleaver, and the talented Kaleena Kiff would play her.

In the series, we also get to meet Eddie's wife, Gertrude, or "Gert" as she is called. Another talented actress, Ellen Maxted, would play Gert. She's an unselfish, doting wife to Eddie's self-absorption, and offers a great contrast to her scheming hubby. Unfortunately, she wouldn't be introduced until late in the first season, and would only appear in eighteen episodes.

Another important change for the series was that Eddie would now have two sons on the show. Edward C. Haskell Jr. aka "Bomber" would be written into the script as away at military school, and he would only appear on a few episodes, and he would be played artfully by our son Christian. The funny thing there was that my wife Sandy and I nicknamed him "The Bomber" when he was just a baby. This was in reference to the Kansas City Bombers roller-skating team. This connection was in keeping with the Connely/Mosher practice of utilizing real life details. I was glad that Brian Levant felt the same way.

My main son, the one who I would most interact with on the show, would now be Fredrick or "Freddie" Haskell, masterfully played by my son Eric. But unlike the MOW, Eric would have some stiff competition to get this role.

> *Brian Levant,*
> *"The part, and the one line, in the movie of the week was a gift. If Eric wanted to do the series, he was going to have to work very hard and go up against seasoned actors in auditions…but he nailed it. And I attributed it to what I called 'The Osmond Focus.'"*

* * *

We shot the first episode of the new series, *Growing Pains,* on August 24, 1984. Just like the MOW, the first couple of shows in the series were designed to get the characters and situations established. And just like on the original series, on Mondays we would do a read through of the script, and then run through it with writers. After the shows started getting completed, we would have lunch, and get to watch the finished shows. We had lots of laughs, and there were many episodes that I found a lot of fun to do. One of these, *Haskells vs. Cleavers,* an episode where Eddie's little league team plays Beaver and Wally's team for the championship, was very memorable to make, on several levels.

For one thing, it was the first show that Brian Levant had ever directed. He had been a veteran writer and a producer for years, but he had never directed. And like everything in life, the first time is always nerve racking, and can often lead to some comical moments.

In the very first scene from the episode, we wasted a lot of film. Not because we had to do numerous takes, but because we did it right…the very first time. When Brian saw how perfectly we all nailed the scene, he exclaimed, "Hey, that was great!"

But saying something is *great* doesn't stop the camera from rolling, it just keeps going until the director yells, "Cut!" Finally, someone realized what was going on and hinted to Brian that he needed to yell, "Cut!" I think he was kind of embarrassed, but we all had a good laugh.

Haskells vs. Cleavers was also one of my favorite "Eddie" type of shows to do, because it showed a human side to Eddie. What was even more memorable about it was the fact that Eddie's vulnerability was due to the fact that he had a tiff with Freddie, so I was able to do it with my own son.

In the end, there is a very touching scene where Eddie hugs Freddie, but then, at the last minute, in vintage Eddie fashion, he still remembers to take down the $20 bill he had tacked up in the dugout. *Heh, heh, heh!*

A lot of the shows also harked back to some of the episodes from the original series. In *A Boy and His Snake*, Freddie is trying to hide his terminally ill boa constrictor from his father, because he cannot deal with the fact that it has to be put down. Freddie enlists the aid of Wally and Beaver's children and asks them to hide the snake in the Cleaver house – which is still June's house. Just like the very first show from the original series, *Captain Jack*, where the young Wally and Beaver hide the pet alligator they bought in the toilet tank, this wasn't the first reptile to be sequestered in the Cleaver home.

The New Leave It to Beaver cast. Front to back: Kipp Marcus, Eric Osmond, John Snee, Barbara Billingsley, Kaleena Kiff, Jerry Mathers, Tony Dow, Janice Kent, Frank Bank, and yours truly. Courtesy of Universal Studios Licensing LLC.

Doing the series also mirrored the fun I had doing the original show, except this time, the ones who were having a blast were my two sons Eric and Christian. They had access to a golf cart to ride around in, and had a great time exploring the back lot and around the studio.

> *Christian Osmond,*
> *"I remember they filmed the TV show Airwolf right*

*across from where we filmed Beaver. Eric and I
would sneak over there and check out the
helicopter."*

*Eric Osmond,
"I remember the first time I went to the studio
commissary and there was a cowboy and an ape-
man standing in line with me. On the wall in the
commissary they also had a picture of our entire
cast displayed, which was pretty awesome."*

By the end of the first season we had an eighty share
on the Disney Channel. I credit everyone involved with
the show for turning out such a superior product on a
tight budget, especially the producers of the show who
had to really innovate to keep our costs down. We were
the first TV show in the US to edit digitally, and the first
show to write our scripts on a computer and print them
ourselves. Still, in Hollywood, it seems that no good
deed can go unpunished, and Disney canceled us after
only one season.

Universal was very upset, but still believed in all of
us. They produced thirteen more episodes and then went
looking for a buyer. We all kept our fingers crossed and
after what seemed like an eternity, our knight in shining
armor finally arrived. He was known popularly as *The
Mouth of the South.*

* * *

TBS media mogul and *Leave It to Beaver* fan, Ted
Turner came to our rescue in 1986 and ordered a
stunning seventy-four episodes of the show, which
would now be titled, *The New Leave It to Beaver.* It was
a great sigh of relief for all of us. For Christian and Eric
it was welcome news as well, but not for the financial

concerns the rest of us had.

> *Eric Osmond,*
> *"Being picked up by TBS was a big deal because it*
> *was huge number of episodes they ordered. To me,*
> *it meant I was going to be able to play around the*
> *back lot of Universal for a couple of more years!"*

Getting picked up also meant that some of the other cast members could realize their dreams as well. Both Tony Dow and Janice Kent would get to direct several episodes, and Tony would get to write one. I was supposed to write an episode, but for various reasons, it never occurred.

So we rolled up our sleeves for the second season and got right to work. The TBS people must have thought that Wally and Mary Ellen needed another mouth to feed, so early in the season we discovered that she was pregnant. I still had my hands full with my two sons, and we finally got to see Christian in action in *A Farewell to Freddie.* In the episode, Eddie had Freddie shipped off to join his brother in military school after he didn't place a bet for his father on a 90-1 long-shot horse that ended up winning.

Freddie arrives and sees that his younger brother is even more of a chip off the old block than he is. "Bomber" runs an extortion/protection racket within the schools hallowed halls that would make the most seasoned of Mafia Dons envious.

Still, Freddie misses home dearly and pines to return to Mayfield. In the end, Eddie begins missing his son as well and shows up at the academy to take him home. He offers the same amnesty to Bomber, but the younger Haskell grins and says that, "He has too good of a gig going here."

I really liked this episode for two reasons: One, it was

the first time all of us got to act together. And two, Eric and Christian each got to show off their renditions of the "Eddie cackle" that we had spent so many hours honing.

A Farewell to Freddie was an emotional Eddie episode, but the one I enjoyed doing the most was *Home For Christmas*. In it, Eddie convinces Freddie to enter a contest to win a Ferrari for him, by sitting up on a radio billboard longer than any of the other contestants. When the contest lasts longer than anyone could have predicted and goes into the holidays, Eddie suffers a crisis of guilt and calls down Freddie from the sign, even though it's down to only him and one other contestant. When Freddie balks and accuses his father of loving a car more than his own son, Eddie unloads with a fusillade of endearment, in terms only a guy like Eddie Haskell can truly appreciate.

EDDIE
"Are you kidding Freddie? I love you more than *Monday Night Football*, more than happy hour, more than long showers, and even more than kick boxing!"

The episode was memorable for Eric as well, though not in the same way.

> *Eric Osmond,*
> *"I remember I was sitting up on this billboard in this coat and it was supposed to be the winter and snowing. They had this fake snow falling down on me. In reality, it was a heat wave and I was baking up there. I think it helped me realize I wanted to be on the post production end of the entertainment industry."*

Of course not all of the emotional Eddie episodes dealt with the turmoil between Freddie and his father. In the episode *Life Without Father,* the actor George Petrie returns to his role as Eddie's estranged father George Haskell. Unbeknownst to Eddie, George is invited to Freddie's sixteenth birthday party. The gloves come off, and Eddie and George really go at it about their mutual disappointment with each other. In the end, Freddie stands up for his father, and George leaves, never to return.

Freddie's defense of his father causes Eddie to get choked up. Again, it is a revealing insight into what makes Eddie tick.

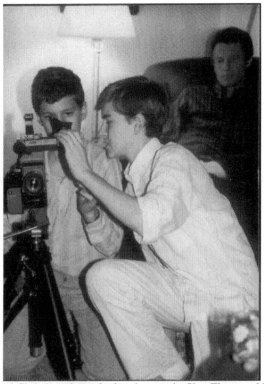

Eric and Christian always had an interest in film. They would make all kinds of movies with their video camera, which they worked very hard to purchase.

There were lots of Eddie shows throughout the run of the series. There was the episode *Murder in Mayfield* where Beaver's son Oliver thinks I am going to kill my wife Gert to collect on her life insurance. And there was a great episode, *Got To Get You Out Of My Life*, co-written by Tony Dow and directed by Brian Levant. In it, the Haskells: Eddie, Freddie, and "Bomber" Eddie Jr. unleash a triple salvo of disruption on the Cleaver's life that has June, Wally, and the Beaver all disowning the Haskell family forever. There is a great dream sequence in the episode that has June Cleaver experiencing a nightmare that has all of her family turning into Eddie Haskells!

At the denouement of *Got To Get You Out Of My Life* Eddie's reputation is salvaged and he is back in the Cleaver's graces when he saves June's house from burning down. The entire Cleaver clan makes it out okay and there are apologies to Eddie, as well as a prodigal son welcoming home.

It's only after everyone steps away though, do we discover that the "fire" was actually a ruse perpetrated by Eddie and Freddie, the latter of whom set smoke bombs off on the top of the Cleaver's roof. *Heh, heh, heh!*

Being an accused murderer, faux arsonist, or con artist were okay, but the one thing I would not have Eddie be is a thief. When one of the scripts called for Eddie to steal his mother-in-law's Social Security check, I drew the line. I refused to go down that path and have Eddie stoop so low. I refused and told them they had to change it. They weren't happy, but the script got re-written.

Besides the cast of regulars, we also tried to bring back as many of the guest stars and recurring stars from the original show. Veronica Cartwright was back as Violet Rutherford, Rusty Stevens reprised his role as

Larry Mondello, and Tiger Fafara was once again "Tooey" Brown.

Of course Eric and Christian really enjoyed some of the newer up and coming stars that we had as guests on the show such as Joaquin Phoenix and Giovanni Ribisi. And they especially liked the young girls such as Christina Applegate, Shannen Doherty and Ami Dolenz, the daughter of Mickey Dolenz.

Seasons two and three seemed to meld together and we were all becoming closer. We had really jelled as a group, and had a lot of fun doing the shows. Just like the original *Leave It to Beaver*, we had no set divas and no conflicts on the set. We really were one big happy family.

> Brian Levant,
> "Stu Shostak, an internet radio program producer and host, is a friend of mine and a huge Leave it to Beaver fan. One time, he sent me a link to a Youtube video that was taken of some "B" roll of when we were making the new show. What I saw was ten minutes of the happiest set I have ever seen in my life. It made me feel I had achieved everything I wanted to by recreating the spirit of the show, and by making it the experience I always wanted it to be."

As much fun as the shows were to make, it seemed we were always working under a dark cloud. There was always the threat of cancellation, and we were always under budget constraints. In fact, there was even a very divisive writer's strike that occurred doing the run of the show. And then, just like in the original show; *Beaver* was going to get moved again.

* * *

Universal had just opened up some studios on the East Coast in Florida. In reality, it wasn't much to speak of, just a couple of sound stages with a chain link fence around them. The suits in the executive suites of Universal must have figured that the studios should be used for something, and so our production was moved down there.

There were some downsides to working in Florida. There was no Colonial Street, like at Universal Studios in Los Angeles, that would serve for the externals of the Cleaver's home on Pine Street. And so the external scenes of the house had to be done inside on a sound stage with fake grass and faux sunlight. A lot of times you had to be very careful walking on the grass, because it wasn't tacked down and it would move and wrinkle up under your feet.

We had a lot of fun on the plane trip down to Florida. And look who is, not surprisingly, goofing off.
Heh, heh, heh.

But there were some upsides as well. The studios treated us very well, giving us unlimited passes to the movies, and plenty of swamp boat rides in the Everglades. Eric and Christian really loved it as well. Eric was now seventeen and had his own convertible and his own apartment. Christian was still too young to be on his own and stayed with me. Still, Christian reveled in the amount of money he was making.

Christian Osmond,
"I had my own car detailing business back in Los Angeles. I'd spend three hours washing and waxing a car just to make $25. Down in Florida, we got $50 a day, just in per diem, to get my McDonalds for the day!"

And so we worked hard and played hard for our fourth and final season. We had lots of great parties, and cast and crew events. One of the things that was very special to all of us, was the fact that Joe Connelly, the co-creator of the original series, saw all of our finished episodes. He had suffered a stroke years before, but his daughter told us that he would watch an episode every night before he went to bed. Joe kept in touch with us, wrote letters to us, and came to all of our parties. He even was there for our 100th episode party, which occurred in Florida just after we wrapped the show *Dads and Grads*.

Dancing with Barbara at our 100th episode party. All of those years complimenting her on her dress finally paid off.

But, just as graduation means an end to your school years, and all the memories they carried with them, after episode 101, we were cancelled. It had been a great run and unfortunately, for reasons too lengthy to explain here, the series never got put into syndication, nor became available on video or DVD.

There would be a *Leave It to Beaver* feature length film that would get made in 1997, and Barbara, Frank, and I would all have cameos in it, but for the most part, it was the end of the line. Jerry would never again play the lovably innocent Beaver, Tony would never again play his protective older brother Wally, and I would never again play America's preeminent bad boy, Edward Clark Haskell. Since 1957, after 32 years, the party was finally over.

Eddie Haskell Trivia answer Chapter 27: The

subtle homage in the MOW "Still The Beaver"was a tribute to Norman Tokar, who directed many of the original Leave It to Beaver shows. In the scene, Wally and Mary Ellen visit the OB/GYN, the sign on the office door reads: "Dr. N. Tokar."

TWENTY-NINE
WRAP-UP

In between the time the MOV premiered and we made the series, the upper brass at LAPD made a decision that would affect me for the rest of my life. They determined that, based upon the trauma I had suffered as a result of the two shooting incidents, that I should be given the opportunity to take an early retirement due to "undue stress suffered in the line of duty."

LAPD was a good job and I worked with a lot of great people. But I honestly wouldn't miss the lousy hours, or putting my life on the line every minute of every day. In the process of writing this book, Christopher J. Lynch and I retraced the route of both shootings. I even stood in the same doorway where my assailant had fired the shots at me at point blank range. I'll admit that being out on the same streets made me incredibly nervous.

My old partner and great friend Henry Lane retired from the police department a few years later, along with Steve Fischer, and a bunch of other guys from deuce watch.

Kim Roderick, the fine young lady that Henry and I looked after while we were on patrol, went on to attend paramedic school at Daniel Freeman Hospital in Los Angeles. She graduated in December 1984, and Henry and I were blessed to be able to attend the ceremony. Since then, she has been honored with numerous awards and recognition. She was the Star of Life for California one year. She's now the EMS Chief for the Palo Alto Fire Department.

One of her stories was even featured on *Rescue 9-1-1* in the early '90s. Her and her crew were also followed in '93 by a local production crew, and have a show on the Discovery Channel, as well as the New York production of *Paramedics* in early 2000s for a one-hour show.

With Kim Roderick in 2014.

On a more negative note, the guy who shot me three times in the doorway is currently on California's Death Row. Unfortunately, after my shooting, since the DA went very light on him, he was given a slap on the wrist, and was out on parole in three years. Within a few months of being released, he killed an innocent man outside of a bar in Pasadena, California in 1985.

Another thing that changed in my life, was that Sandy and I moved from our original home in Sun Valley. Our two sons were growing up before our eyes, and we needed bigger digs. Besides needing the space, Sandy had been a horse person all of her life and I wanted to be able to provide that for her by getting us a place in horse country. The only problem was, there were no houses in the area that we could afford, but there was a vacant lot. We purchased it and then we only needed to put a house on it. The cost of the lot had us pretty tapped out, and so we couldn't afford the construction cost of building a brand new home, even if grandpa Purdy and I did a lot of the work. But I knew that there was more than one way to skin a cat.

We found an existing house that had been deeded to a church after the owner died. The church wanted the property cleared to expand its house of worship, and they didn't care about the house. So we purchased the house with the intention of moving it, all the way from Huntington Beach – seventy miles away!

It took three entire days for the house to arrive and when it did, we noticed something was missing, the master bedroom. The church had been so anxious to get the lot cleared to start expanding, they mistakenly demolished the master bedroom of the home. Oh well, just like I had to expand our doorframe to make our oversized front door fit, I knew I could tackle this obstacle as well.

The end result is that we now have a wonderful home on three-quarters of an acre and Sandy has her dream of having her horses on our own property. She has two, and their names are Kimi and Banner.

In addition to the house we live in, we began

snapping up as many houses that we could as investments. Some of these we would flip to make a profit, and others we would keep as rentals for retirement income. Eric and Christian also got into the act, and were able to take the money they made from working on the series and purchase homes as investments also. They were so young when they bought their first homes that Sandy and I had to co-sign for them.

There were some sad times as well, however. My mother, Pearl Osmond, passed away in 1984 at the age of 65. She was a strong woman and a beacon in my life. I will always be indebted to her, as well as to my father who followed her to eternity, six years later. He was 78 years of age, and a good man whom I had become very close to.

Grandpa Purdy passed on in 1994 at the ripe old age of 85, and Sandy's mother was with us until 2001 when she departed. Both of them had been extremely good to our sons, and they had treated me as one of their own.

But life marches on and renews itself, and Sandy and I could not be prouder of our two sons Eric and Christian. Besides blessing us with some wonderful grandchildren, both of them followed their passions and have become very successful professionals.

Christian Osmond is now Dr. Christian Osmond. He is a graduate of the University of Wisconsin's School of Veterinary Medicine. After he earned his doctorate degree in veterinary medicine, he completed an internship in medicine and surgery at the Veterinary Medical and Surgical Group in Ventura, California and is now considered one of the top veterinary surgeons in the State of California.

Eric took a different path, but not one that would have been a surprise to any of us. Ever since he was young, he had an interest in making films. He and

Christian actually saved up half of the money so they could get a video camera for Christmas one year. Almost as soon as *The New Leave It to Beaver* series ended, Eric enrolled in the USC School of Film. He graduated in 1993 after finishing with his studies in only 3 1/2 years so that he could work on *The Flintstones* as a production assistant. Since then, he's worked on *Thor, Despicable Me 2, The Lorax,* and *The Minion Movie.*

Sandy, Christian, Eric, and myself at Eric's graduation from USC Film School.

My older brother Dayton decided to have another go in the industry as well, although not as an actor. After the helicopter debacle, he went back to work for the studios and ended up doing special effects, including working for Tony Dow when Tony directed the TV series *Babylon 5.*

Speaking of Tony Dow, after he got his feet wet directing some episodes on the revival series, he decided he enjoyed working on that side of the camera. He ended up having a long, successful run directing such shows as *The New Lassie, Harry and the Hendersons,* and *Coach.* He eventually left acting to pursue his other passion, which is sculpting. He's a well-renowned artist, and has had some of his work on display at the Louvre Museum in France.

After the end of the series, Jerry Mathers continued working in films and television roles. In the 1990s, he guest starred on episodes of *Parker Lewis Can't Lose*, *Vengeance Unlimited,* and *Diagnosis Murder*. In 1998, Mathers released his memoirs, *And Jerry Mathers As The Beaver*. And in 2007, he made his Broadway debut with a starring role as Wilbur Turnblad in the Tony winning best musical *Hairspray* at the Neil Simon Theater. In 2010, Jerry became the national spokesperson for PhRMA and their Partnership for Prescription Assistance program. This organization helps uninsured and financially struggling patients obtain prescription medicines for low, or no, cost.

Brian Levant, our producer, director, and the developer of the revival series, is still busy making movies including *Beethoven, The Flintstones, Jingle all the Way*, and the soon to be released *Vanilla Gorilla*. Brian works very closely with our son Eric.

Barbara Billingsley unfortunately passed away in October of 2010. She was an absolutely adorable woman whom we all loved.

Another sad parting was Frank Bank's death in April of 2013. Of all of the members of the original cast, I was closest to Frank and his passing affected me deeply.

Frank Bank and I always remained close through the years.
Courtesy of Universal Studios Licensing LLC.

As far as myself, after the series ended, I pretty much gave up for good on acting. I would do an occasional cameo role if it happens to come along, but that's about it. These days I mostly work maintaining my rentals, and doing occasional public appearances.

I also volunteer at my local American Legion Post 520 in Sun Valley where I'm an officer. Eight years ago, I took over the publication of our post newsletter and found it to be very lacking. Basically it was nothing more than a calendar of the post events, past and future.

I was reading the newspaper one day and read the obituary of a gentleman who had recently passed. The man had served in the navy and was a surviving member of the USS Indianapolis, which had been sunk by a Japanese sub after delivering the atomic bomb at the end of WWII. The story was so gripping and inspiring, I decided to write it into the post newsletter.

Everyone at the post loved it, so before I knew it, I was scouring the internet and obituaries for more stories of unsung heroes. My collection of stories eventually became a book, *Above And Beyond*, which I recently published and is available at Amazon as a print or e-book.

My book on military history, a homage to those who went,
Above And Beyond.

It's very important to me to do what I can to honor
and support our veterans, including even those who have
made a mistake or two in their lives. I recently learned of
a special group of inmates at a prison north of Los
Angeles that perform fundraisers and use the money to

support organizations such as the Blue Star Mothers. The Blue Star Mothers then use the funds to send care packages to our troops overseas.

With my background in law enforcement, I found that I had some conflicted feelings about the group, but in the end, I realized that they had served their country, and now, even though they were incarcerated, they were still serving it by supporting our men and women in uniform. I requested a visit to meet with them and I was warmly received. I donated copies of *Above And Beyond* and they were put into the prison library so that everyone could read them.

Some members of the V.E.T.S. group posing in front of a mural they painted inside the prison. The mural honors our military men and women and ever branch of the service is represented. It was very special to be able to visit them.

I am a proud American and an unabashed patriot. And as long as I am alive, I will continue to support our military men and women, even if some of them are more like Eddie Haskell than I ever was. And speaking of Eddie…

THIRTY
EDDIE, ON EDDIE

In a line from a *Leave It to Beaver* script in 1958, Wally informs his younger brother that, "A kid like Eddie Haskell only comes along about once in a couple hundred years."

Maybe there was only one Eddie Haskell in the fictional town of Mayfield at that moment in time, but there are plenty of Mayfields in the world, and plenty more "Eddies."

Throughout the years, Eddie Haskell has meant a lot of things to a lot of people, and a lot of people have known at least one in their life. Eddie is your co-worker, your brother in law, or the mechanic who fixes your car.

He was the consummate suck up, schemer, troublemaker, and con artist. Because of this, he was and still is, the reference point for many people to use as a warning to others; "Be careful of that guy, he's like an Eddie Haskell."

And more than one cautious mother has used this gold standard for rotten kids to warn their children; "I don't want you to play with that kid, he seems like an

Eddie Haskell to me."

Interestingly, I know of one mother who I had never known to use the term, my own mother Pearl. In all of my years, she never used it to describe someone she didn't trust. And even when Dayton and I would get into mischief, she never accused either of us of acting like Eddie Haskell.

Political foes and media talking heads love to channel Eddie Haskell, and foes as disparate as Rush Limbaugh and Barrack Obama have each used the term to deride their opponents. Once, Rush Limbaugh compared Bill Clinton to Eddie Haskell. I'm no fan of Bill Clinton, and I contacted the program to complain, explaining that I'm the real Eddie Haskell and that I don't like being compared to Bill Clinton. Rush Limbaugh happily issued an on-air apology for insulting me.

Sports fans get into the act as well, and when a Kobe Bryant or Lebron James complain about a foul call, the peanut gallery loves to tweet that they are acting like Eddie Haskell.

A famous comedian who was agonizing over his daughter's recent entry into the dating world, complained to a talk show host that, "I just hope she doesn't come home with some guy who's an Eddie Haskell."

Image courtesy of Universal Studios Licensing LLC
*Even Dow Chemical couldn't help but take a swipe at Eddie
Haskell with this pesticide ad.*

The term Eddie Haskell is listed twice in the *Urban Dictionary,* as well as some mainstream dictionaries. Eddie Haskell is the topic of a business blog related to recruitment and hiring, warning businesses to, "Watch out for Eddie Haskell."

Psychology Today Magazine published an article in 2011 titled, "Bullies And The Eddie Haskell Effect."

Google has a search term for "The Eddie Haskell Syndrome" which returns over 2 million results, including a sermon from a Minister at a church in Washington state, "A Parable Of Eddie Haskell Syndrome."

There are two Eddie Haskell bands, and there was once an Eddie Haskell restaurant.

Throughout this book, I have written at length about my two sons, Eric and Christian, who could rightly claim that they are the true "sons of Eddie Haskell." But one famous TV producer came up with his own version of the "son of Eddie." Matt Groening, the creator of *The Simpson*, stated that when he watched *Leave It to Beaver* as a child, he would "Vibrate with happiness every time Eddie Haskell came on the screen," and that he wanted to create a show around a bad character. And that bad character is Bart Simpson, whom Groening describes as, "The son of Eddie Haskell."

Other people may have had a firm idea as to what Eddie Haskell represented to them, but to me he is a dichotomy.

There was the Eddie who was my biggest enemy, at least in Hollywood. After the show ended, I found myself typecast and unable to get anything except for other "Eddie" parts. It was like a millstone around my neck, or a scarlet letter. I would walk into an interview and there it was; the same expression of recognition, of knowing that they know who you are. And if the casting agent, who sees thousands of people in a year remembered you instantly, then the millions of people who let you inhabit their living rooms every week could certainly never forget you. Being typecast is just about as close to a death sentence in Hollywood as anything.

There was also the Eddie who kept me out of undercover work on the police force when my cover was blown with the screaming story; "Eddie Haskell is now an LAPD officer!"

And then of course, there were the rumors that I had to deal with, especially the John Holmes one that got me called onto the carpet as a policeman, the only time I ever had to report to internal affairs in the eighteen years I was in the police department. Not to mention of course, the embarrassing effects it had on my wife Sandy.

But then, there was the other Eddie. The one who helped get *The New Leave It to Beaver* series off the ground. The one who allowed me to work with my old friends again, and especially, to act with my two sons.

And then there are the countless "Eddie perks."

I've been interviewed hundreds of times and have done numerous personal appearances. I've been made an honorary mayor and police chief of at least thirty cities throughout the United States. I've ridden in parades, helped open shopping centers, and signed thousands of autographs and photographs at memorabilia shows. Every day when I go to the mailbox, there are fan letters telling me how much they love the show and the character.

With Charlton Heston.

I've been invited to numerous celebrity golf tournaments, I've shot skeet with Charlton Heston, and I was invited up onto the stage of the Grand Ol' Opry – both venues. I got to enjoy a drink with Bill Monroe, the undisputed father of Bluegrass. I water-skied with the

Cypress Gardens water-ski team, and I was the guest of General "Stormin" Norman Schwarzkopf at a charity quail hunt in Oklahoma. And although I have no quarrel with hunters, I no longer shoot animals and simply walked alongside the general.

My family and I were guests of the astronauts, and watched a space shuttle launch as VIPs. Later, I was honored to have dinner with the legendary Apollo 13 astronaut, Jim Lovell.

Meeting astronaut Jim Lovell was a great honor for me.

But one of the greatest of all perks was when my wife, her father, and I were invited with a select group to have dinner at the White House with Ronald Reagan. We had a private tour and it was an experience I'll always treasure. I guess even the "Gipper" was an Eddie fan. Later, I gave a gift of two Mayfield letterman's sweaters to the president and Mrs. Reagan.

In summary, since I was fourteen years old, Eddie Haskell has always been with me. He is, in some ways, my shadow. He follows me everywhere, and I can't shake him, no matter how fast I run, or where I go. And while there have been some up and down times with him, in the end, Eddie Haskell has been very good to me. He's brought me fame, some fortune, and some of the most amazing times in my life.

Eddie was, is, and always will be, my friend.

ABOUT CHRISTOPHER J. LYNCH

Los Angeles native Christopher J. Lynch has written for numerous local and national publications. A lover of crime fiction, he has also published short stories and is the author of the *One Eyed Jack* series of books about a professional blackmailer. The debut novel in the series, was a 2013 Shamus Award finalist.

When he's not writing, Christopher enjoys distance cycling and mountain climbing. His climbs have led him to the summits of Mount Whitney, Mount Shasta, Mount Kilimanjaro in Africa, and Mount Kala Patar in Nepal. He recently completed a trek to Mount Everest Base Camp.

He considers the greatest accomplishment of his life to be the training and leading of eleven blind hikers to the summit of 10,000 foot Mount Baldy, the highest point in Los Angeles County, and the third highest point in Southern California. A documentary film is being made of the adventure: http://www.baldyfortheblind.com

Christopher's website is http://www.christopherjlynch.com

Made in the USA
Columbia, SC
19 October 2023